BEFORE THE STORM

LOVE IN THE ADIRONDACKS

JEN TALTY

JUPITER PRESS

This book is a work of fiction. Names, characters, places, and incidents are products of the author's imagination or used fictitiously. Any resemblance to actual events or locales or persons living or dead is entirely coincidental.

Copyright © 2024 by Jen Talty All rights reserved.

No part of this work may be used, stored, reproduced or transmitted without written permission from the publisher except for brief quotations for review purposes as permitted by law. This book is licensed for your personal enjoyment only. This book may not be re-sold or given away to other people. If you would like to share this book with another person, please purchase an additional copy for each recipient. If you're reading this book and did not purchase it, or it was not purchased for your use only, please purchase your own copy.

PRAISE FOR JEN TALTY

"Deadly Secrets is the best of romance and suspense in one hot read!" *NYT Bestselling Author Jennifer Probst*

"A charming setting and a steamy couple heat up the pages in a suspenseful story I couldn't put down!" *NY Times and USA today Bestselling Author Donna Grant*

"Jen Talty's books will grab your attention and pull you into a world of relatable characters, strong personalities, humor, and believable storylines. You'll laugh, you'll cry, and you'll rush to get the next book she releases!" Natalie Ann USA Today Bestselling Author

"I positively loved *In Two Weeks*, and highly recommend it. The writing is wonderful, the story is fantastic, and the characters will keep you coming back for more. I can't wait to get my hands on future installments of the NYS Troopers series." *Long and Short Reviews*

"*In Two Weeks* hooks the reader from page one. This is a fast paced story where the development of the romance grabs you emotionally and the suspense keeps you sitting on the edge of your chair. Great characters, great writing, and a believable plot that can be a warning to all of us." *Desiree Holt, USA Today Bestseller*

"*Dark Water* delivers an engaging portrait of wounded hearts as the memorable characters take you on a healing journey of love. A mysterious death brings danger and intrigue into the drama, while sultry passions brew into a believable plot that melts the reader's heart. Jen Talty pens an entertaining romance that grips the heart as the colorful and dangerous story unfolds into a chilling ending." *Night Owl Reviews*

"This is not the typical love story, nor is it the typical mystery. The characters are well rounded and interesting." *You Gotta Read Reviews*

"*Murder in Paradise Bay* is a fast-paced romantic thriller with plenty of twists and turns to keep you guessing until the end. You won't want to miss this one..." *USA Today bestselling author Janice Maynard*

BOOK DESCRIPTION

***Running was the only thing she'd ever known—
and she wasn't afraid to go straight through the
storm.***

In the aftermath of military service, Phoenix Snow,
once adept at burying his emotions, finds himself
adrift in his own life. Now pursuing a new path
alongside his brothers, he finds himself at a
crossroads. His journey takes an unexpected turn
when fate introduces him to Janelle, a woman
haunted by a harrowing past.

Janelle fled the clutches of a polygamous cult that
stole her innocence and shattered her spirit. Despite
the shadows of her past lurking at every turn, she
presses onward, driven by the hope of a brighter

future. But fate has different plans and Janelle is forced to confront her deepest fears. With her past threatening to unravel her newfound peace, she must find the courage not only to embrace love but also to confront the demons that have plagued her for years, all while safeguarding those who share her plight.

For Kimberly. Thanks for taking the journey. I can't do this without you.

And for Kris. Thanks for being my comic relief during the writing process of this one. I couldn't have gotten through the final push without the laughter.

For Kimberly Thoene, for taking the journey. I can't do this work without you.

And for Kai & Eli — for hanging on, coming with, through every mm,p,o,s,o,q of each one. I couldn't have gotten enough Bachhof push without the laughter.

PROLOGUE

THREE YEARS AGO...

A Small Town in Arizona

Sister Aura Margret Bueller folded her hands in her lap and lowered her head as she did before every meal. Her heart hammered in her chest like it never had before. She was no longer peaceful. She no longer wanted this life. It wasn't her calling.

It never had been.

Her life had been a lie and it had been spoon-fed to her by her father.

Brother Jim, her spiritual husband—as he was called in her culture—sat at the head of the table while her sister wives occupied either the seat next to her or across from her, doing the same thing.

They were obedient wives, unlike Janelle, who had begun to question the doctrine and the very fiber of their way of life.

That hadn't gone over well with her husband and especially her father.

The twelve children who still lived at home were all situated at another table except the two babies. They were in bassinets near their birth mothers.

Although all the wives were considered moms. They all helped to take care of and raise the children. It was their duty as women under the watchful eye of the Lord.

But Aura didn't feel like a mother.

Nor did she want to be one.

Not at twenty-three.

She'd been pregnant four times. Three miscarriages and one stillbirth. Brother Jim said she was a complete and utter failure as a wife. He had been so disappointed in her inability to give him another child that he'd stopped visiting her and told her she needed to pray harder and that when God was ready for her to achieve her true calling, he'd come to Brother Jim and make his wishes be known.

Immediately, she stopped praying altogether.

If there was a God, she no longer believed.

She had no faith at all. Not in the religion that she was born and raised with. Not in polygamy, something she once thought she valued and respected. Not in her family.

And certainly not in the head of her church, who happened to be her father.

"Amen," Jim said. However, she had no idea what words he had uttered before, nor did she care.

There was only one thing she cared about, and that was getting out of this godforsaken hellhole.

"Sister Aura, did you have a nice visit with your father today?" her husband asked. The sound of his voice made her shiver with disgust.

She stared at the plate of food, her stomach in knots. She'd spent her entire life living in this compound and doing her best to live and breathe the doctrine. The only times she'd ever stepped foot outside the walls had been when she'd gone to the hospital during complications of childbirth three months ago.

That's when she'd met the woman who had put a single thought in her brain that she couldn't get out.

"Yes, Brother Jim," she said, keeping her gaze lowered. He'd blamed her for not having a strong enough faith.

Well, he wasn't wrong about her belief system.

That died the moment her father had told her she

was to marry a forty-year-old man when she'd only been seventeen.

Oddly, it wasn't the fact that he had other wives. That hadn't bothered her at all. The idea of sister wives had been normal and something she planned on living. Her mother had been one of three wives. For the first ten years of Aura's life, she believed the polygamy lifestyle had been one of choice. One that a woman chose for herself when she came of age. And that was probably true for many in her type of faith.

However, shortly after her biological mother passed, her father took on a much younger wife and a fundamental shift in the church began.

Although, at first, that didn't even seem weird. Ten years wasn't that big of a deal between a husband and his wife.

But it was the next wife her father took that made Aura sick to her stomach. She'd only been sixteen and, to date, had given her father three children.

Young wives now seemed to be a thing, and the mothers were going along with it. Encouraging it, even.

It wasn't right and Aura didn't need the outside world to tell her that.

"What was the topic of discussion?" Brother Jim asked as he dug into his food.

Aura swallowed. She did not want to have this discussion. It made her want to vomit. "Obedience," she managed to choke out.

"Your sister wives have informed me that you didn't finish your chores and that you allowed some children a treat when they weren't supposed to have one." He arched a brow. "I'm not sure you've learned your lesson yet."

If that meant he would stay with one of his other wives, then she was never going to learn. "My father told me to continue to pray for God's wisdom and forgiveness."

"Your father is a wise man," Brother Jim said. "It's why he's the leader of our church. Perhaps you should retire to your room." He took her plate before she could even take a nibble.

"Yes, Brother Jim." She stood, resting her napkin on the table.

"We will discuss all that has transpired in the morning."

She nodded before scurrying off through the family room, down the long corridor, and into the sanctuary of her room. It was the only personal space she was allowed, except Brother Jim could invade it at any time.

Quickly, she found the cell phone that Anne

Marie had given her and with shaky hands, she sent the message.

Aura: *If I'm going to leave, it has to be now.*

Anne Marie: *We'll be outside the compound in fifteen minutes.*

Aura couldn't believe she was going to go through with it. When they met months ago, Anne Marie told her she'd help whenever Aura was ready. Now, all Aura had to do was get out unnoticed.

She peeked her head out the door. The family continued with dinner. They would all be obedient, no one daring to move without permission from the head of the family. This would give her a few minutes to climb out her window and race down the streets.

Hopefully unseen.

The one thing she could count on in her community was that everyone did the same things at the same time. No one would be around. Or at least, no one should be out and about.

As quietly as she could, she lifted the windowpane and hiked up her long dress. The drop down was farther than she anticipated and she twisted her ankle. She hobbled down the road, ignoring the pain.

The front gates were kept locked. She was told that was for their safety, but she knew better. It was to keep them prisoners. However, she'd stolen a set of keys from her father. Her heart pounded as she searched for the one that would unlock the gates from hell.

A vehicle rolled to a stop and Anne Marie rolled down the window and waved. "Hurry. There're cameras. It will only be minutes before someone knows you're gone."

"How do you know that?" She pulled at the heavy metal and ran as fast as she could to the open car door.

And her freedom.

"Not our first rodeo." Anne Marie glanced out the window before rolling it back up.

Aura had known about other sister wives who had left. They were sinners. They had a first-class ticket to hell and weren't welcome back. They had lost their spot in heaven. They had lost their place with God. With their husbands. And they never got to see their children again.

Those who did return were never treated the same way again.

Well, she was never going to show her face in this compound, much less the state of Arizona again.

"Go," Anne Marie said to the driver, a man Aura had never seen.

"What now?" The gravity of what she'd done began to sink in like a brick plummeting to the bottom of the ocean. She had no real education outside of what the church's doctrine had taught. She had no clue as to what the outside world was really like except that according to her father, it was evil and filled with Satan's work.

"We'll take you to a safe house in New Mexico. You'll get a new identity. Learn some life skills. From there, you'll be on your own," the man said, glancing over his shoulder. "Whatever you do, don't go back. It will be tempting because life outside of what you know is going to be hard. But I promise it will be better than the life you could ever have inside those walls."

"How do you know that?" she asked.

"I didn't live there, but I grew up in a place like it. My mom escaped with me when I was fourteen. Best decision she ever made and now I do this, helping girls, boys, and women like you."

Anne Marie reached back and took her hand. "He saved me." She gave Aura a weak smile. "I was in a church much like yours. I wanted out and I found Jason, but two days before I was to make my big escape, the entire compound moved in the middle of the night. It was another four weeks before Jason found me."

"I was determined. I wasn't going to let her suffer anymore. Her spiritual husband was far worse than yours," Jason said. "Her group has been disbanded, but other religious sects always pop up and move around."

Aura understood that. Her family had moved, all in the name of being closer to God. But it had more to do with the fact that the state of Utah didn't agree with plural marriage.

"Not all of these polygamy compounds are like this one," the man said. "Many of them simply want to practice plural marriage in peace. But when they start marrying off young children or hold women in marriages against their will, that's when they need to be stopped and this one has been on our radar for a while. But we need people to talk."

"No. No. No." Aura shook her head. "I can't do that. You don't know what will—"

"I'm not asking you to," the man said.

Anne Marie handed her a packet. "However, if you ever do want to talk or speak up, inside that envelope is how you can reach us. But right now, our priority is to make sure you're safe."

"Thank you." Tears filled her eyes.

The man met her gaze in the rearview mirror. "No need. This is my calling. Now settle in and get some sleep. We have a long drive ahead of us."

Aura stared out the window, fiddling with her knee-length hair. Cutting it short would be the first thing she did in her new life.

1

Phoenix Snow snagged his coffee and made his way to the deck of the Blue Moon. He sucked in a deep breath, letting the cool spring air fill his lungs. The bite of winter had finally given way to warmer temperatures. A few boats lined the docks, ready for the promise of summer.

"Hey, boss." Veronica, the hostess, scurried across the wood floor.

Two weeks ago, it was covered with three inches of snow. Today, the sun shone bright and the weatherman predicted it could reach a high of sixty.

Not bad for early April.

However, anything could happen in Lake George, New York.

"What's up?" Phoenix kept his gaze on the glasslike waters. He loved mornings like this. Cool, crisp, and peaceful. It's why he and his brothers had gravitated to this very spot. It gave them everything they had ever wanted in their second career.

A bar and restaurant to call their own.

A place to put down roots.

And for Nelson and Maverick—well, they had found love and family.

Phoenix certainly didn't begrudge his brothers, their wives, or children. He adored his nieces and nephew. They were the most incredible gifts. He spent as much time with them as he could.

He also worked more lately than his brothers so they could spend quality time with their children.

Having a family hadn't been on Phoenix's radar. Becoming a husband or father hadn't been something he aspired to achieve. He'd never given it much thought, except to tell the women he dated he wasn't interested or looking for love. It wasn't for him. Not because he didn't believe in the concept but because he didn't want to be tied down. He liked the freedom to come and go as he pleased. He didn't want to ask permission to go have a beer with his brothers.

Not that they had to ask their wives, but not everyone was Hensley or Brandi.

"The ad for the new waitress-hostess starts running today, and I hung a sign up in the window."

Veronica leaned against the railing. "I also put up your flyer for your rental on the board by the door."

"Thanks, I appreciate it." He raised his mug and sipped the bitter brew.

"Are you sure you want to rent your garage apartment?"

He laughed. "You've been talking with my brothers, haven't you?"

"Actually, your two sisters-in-law."

"Wonderful. The whole family's in on it." He let out a long sigh. This past winter, he'd spent all his spare time fixing up the space over his detached garage. It gave him something to do while his brothers focused on their children.

So much had changed in the last year and Phoenix needed something to hold his attention. Dating had started to bore him, so this project gave him something to do and occupied his time while he re-evaluated his life.

"They just don't understand it." Veronica cocked her head. "Not to put my nose where it doesn't belong, but it's not like you need the extra cash."

He turned. "You should see this place. Even Doug and Jim are impressed."

"I heard they helped a little."

Phoenix nodded. "Doug did the design and they both came over and worked with me on what was above my pay grade. For a small studio, it came out nice. I thought about doing short-term rentals. But I don't really want to deal with people in and out. So, I thought maybe I could at least find a summer rental."

"I'm just surprised considering how private you are." Veronica rubbed her round belly. She was five months pregnant. It was going to suck when she took her maternity leave. She was more than a hostess. She was their best employee-manager and he would bend over backward to give her whatever she needed during this pregnancy.

"It's not like I'm going to live with whoever I rent it to." He arched a brow. "I'm going to be incredibly picky about who gets that space. Don't you worry."

"I'm not. But if you ask your mom, all you need is a good woman in your life." She smiled. "And on that note, I'm going to skedaddle. The morning crowd is twice as big as it was yesterday."

"Summer's almost here." He squeezed her biceps. "Whoever we hire will help take some pressure off you."

"I appreciate that. Thank you."

"Uncle Phoenix!" a little girl's voice tickled his ears.

Immediately, he smiled. He set his mug on the railing and squatted, spreading his arms wide, waiting for Ashley to come flying into them. "Well, hello there, sweet girl. What are you doing here this morning?"

"Daddy promised me an egg san-wish before pre-kool." She leaped into his arms, hugging him tight, kissing his cheek. She palmed his face and frowned. "Cole's still sick and Mommy had to stay home with him."

"I'm sorry your little brother doesn't feel well, but what a special treat for you." He stood, giving her a good twirl. "And me. I love getting to see you first thing. It makes my day better."

"Hey, little brother." Maverick slapped his back. "I saw the flyer on the board. You're really going to rent that place out?"

"I have to ask. Why does everyone care?"

Maverick chuckled. "I don't. I just don't understand." He held up his hand. "And only because you've been acting weird all winter."

Phoenix set Ashley on the floor and patted her head. "Hey, kiddo, go get Veronica and she'll get you and your dad a couple of sandwiches to go. Come right back though, okay?"

"Sure thing, Uncle Phoenix." She poked her father in the stomach. "Don't lecture him on women."

"Out of the mouths of babes." Phoenix shook his head. "So, that's why everyone has their panties in a wad."

"We're used to a steady rotation of ladies. At least one or two a year. You haven't dated anyone since Hensley and I got married." He leaned over, resting his forearms on the railing. "Not that I want to see you going from one fling to the next, but you don't seem yourself."

Phoenix raked his hand through his hair. "I literally just had this conversation with Mom and Dad two weeks ago. I'm getting tired of it."

"But you didn't tell them anything, which I get. Mom can be overbearing at times and ever since I adopted my kids and Nelson's little girl was born, she's been pushing you hard." Maverick stood tall, tapping the center of his chest. "But it's me you're talking to right now and I know something is going on with you. Talk to me."

Needing a jolt of caffeine, Phoenix downed half his coffee. Normally, he loved winters. He and his brothers would hit the slopes at the local ski resorts. They would go snowmobiling. Ice fishing. Or simply hang out.

This past winter, while they did those things, not a single trip had been taken, and those activities were few and far between. Phoenix didn't resent his brothers or their families. Far from it. He relished in their love. He really did.

But he missed the closeness.

He hated to admit it, but he was lonely.

He wasn't sure he wanted what they had, but he wanted something different.

"Come on, man. What's going on? Why won't you confide in me?"

Shit. Time to rip off the fucking Band-Aid. Phoenix hadn't wanted to do this, but he knew if one of his brothers pushed him hard enough or called him out point-blank, he'd spill the beans. He'd have to. They meant the world to him and he wouldn't bullshit them. "I don't want you to feel bad or think I'm jealous, because I'm not. It's just that everything has changed. Honestly, for the better. I'm truly happy for you and Nelson." He pointed to one of the windows to the restaurant's main room where Ashley had perched herself at the bar, waiting patiently for her and her daddy's food. "Those kids are amazing and I love spending time with them. Hensley and Brandi are two of the best women outside Mom I know. But all of that has changed the dynamics between the three of us and I need to figure out my new normal." He shrugged.

"That doesn't explain your lack of dating." Maverick tilted his head. "Did something happen that we all missed?"

"God, no," Phoenix said. "I got bored. And

frankly, tired of being called the last good catch in our family."

"Seriously?"

"Oh yeah. The last girl I dated was super excited to be with the last available Snow brother. It was weird."

Maverick laughed. "I'm sorry. That's not funny."

"Trust me, it's hilarious," Phoenix said. "Look. I get that outside of family gatherings, I've been acting differently. I'm just responding to changes in the family and finding my place."

"Can I ask you a question about dating without you getting pissed?"

"Sure."

"Are you bored because you're tired of playing the game and would like to settle down finally?"

"Now you sound like Mom." Phoenix had spent the entire winter contemplating that question. He saw how happy his brothers were and wondered if there was something to a life partner. Only, he'd never felt anything particularly special with any one person. It was always about living in the moment. Having a good time. His focus had always been his career in the military.

After that, opening Blue Moon with his brothers.

Now that they had families, Phoenix had to admit, he felt a little lost.

"I don't mean to. But I have noticed you're a little withdrawn lately. Nelson's noticed it too," Maverick said. "I'm checking in. No different than what you did with me so many times."

"That's fair and reasonable." There hadn't been a time in Phoenix's life where he and his brothers hadn't been in tune with each other. His brothers—and his parents—were his lifeline. If he could, he'd walk on water for them, and they would do the same. He appreciated that his brothers had given him space and cared enough to say something. "But I'm fine. Just trying to figure out what I want to do."

"Hensley has a few single friends. One of them she's dying to fix you up with."

"Yeah, I'm well aware." He downed his last sip of coffee. "But no, thank you."

"Why not?"

"Because she's looking to set me up with someone in a forever way and while I'm re-evaluating some things in my life, I still don't believe I'm cut out for that and I wouldn't want to be the guy who hurt one of Hensley's besties."

"Why are you hell-bent on being alone?" Maverick held up his hand. "The last time we had a real conversation about you and long-term commitment, all you had to say was that you had no desire to be married. That was a much different answer from when we were younger and deployed all the time."

Phoenix had no idea how to explain his emotions because he didn't completely understand them. The only thing he knew for sure was that he'd never been in love. He had no idea what that felt like. Only what it looked like. He couldn't say he was afraid of being in love with a woman or the responsibility that brought. However, he did like the freedom to come and go whenever he pleased. That would change if he had a steady person. He would have to think about someone else's feelings and he could be an incredibly selfish human.

"It's not that," Phoenix said. If there was anyone he could be totally raw with, it was his brothers. He didn't open up as often lately. Not because he didn't want to, but because they had other responsibilities and he didn't want to add to that burden. "I'm finding myself at a crossroads. I'm feeling grounded. This is home and we've never had roots firmly planted." He waved his hand toward the lake. "I can't imagine living anywhere else. Ever."

"Neither can I."

"I've dated so many different types of women. All walks of life, from the sophisticated businesswoman to biker chicks. Skinny girls to heavyset ladies.

Blondes, brunettes, redheads. Tall, short, and everything between. I don't have a type. If I ever did consider looking for something more, I wouldn't even know where to begin."

"That's the best bullshit I've ever heard." Maverick shook his head. "A type isn't always about looks." He placed his hand over his chest. "They're about what's in the heart and you, little brother, most certainly have a type when it comes to that."

"Oh really. This I have to hear."

Maverick smiled. It was wide and kid-like. As if he'd walked into a toy store with Mom and Dad's credit card and been told he could max it out. "You like a woman with a quiet soul. Someone who likes reading. Sitting by a fire and enjoying a good sunrise or sunset. Someone who likes outdoor things. You'd want a person who isn't needy but needs you. A person who can take care of themselves but is willing to be vulnerable and capable of asking for help. But you need a person who understands that your family is a package deal." Maverick put his hand up. "The problem is, you've only dated girls who fall into two categories. Emotionally unavailable or clingy as fuck."

Phoenix couldn't deny that last statement. It was as if he went from one extreme to the next, always believing he preferred the woman who kept her distance, but never feeling as though there was anything but decent sex.

That wasn't enough to sustain even a fling for more than a few weeks or months.

And the ones who demanded his full attention?

Way too much fucking work.

"You do realize that's so vague." Phoenix jerked his chin. "Here comes a little devil with the smile of an angel."

"That's the best descriptor of my daughter." Maverick turned, scooping up Ashley. "Ready to go to school?"

"Yes, Daddy." She held up the bag. "Mommy's gonna be mad we ate in the car."

"I think it will be okay this one time." Maverick checked his watch. "We better get going. We're gonna be late." He nodded. "I'll be back in twenty, but I'm gonna have to scoot out to go get her and bring her home."

"No worries. Nelson's coming in for the lunch crowd and will stay through dinner."

"I'll help close tonight." He set Ashley down. "Say goodbye to your uncle."

Ashley wrapped her arms around Phoenix's legs, staring up at him with her bright-blue eyes. "I love you."

"Right back at you, beautiful."

Phoenix followed his brother and niece into the main room of the restaurant and bar. He waved as they strolled out the front door.

His pulse sped up as a young woman with shoulder-length dark hair, wearing loose-fitting jeans, tennis sneakers, and a bulky brown sweater waltzed inside. She tugged at her oversized purse, glancing around.

Veronica greeted her with a smile and showed her to a high-top table in the bar area.

Phoenix swallowed. Hard. The young woman was stunningly beautiful. Her almond-colored eyes seemed to hide a world of hurt. He had no idea why he thought that, but something about her gaze told him that she'd seen things in her short life.

He raced over to the bar and grabbed a water. "I've got this," he said to the waitress in charge of the table. One of the things he and his brothers enjoyed doing was engaging with all the customers.

Especially new ones.

This fell under that category.

"Good morning." He placed the water on the table. "I'm Phoenix. I own Blue Moon. Welcome."

"Thank you." She glanced up from the menu and blinked.

Damn. Those fucking eyes. They were more gold than almond. He could get lost gazing in them if he wasn't careful. "I haven't seen you in here before. First time?"

She nodded.

"Can I get you a coffee? A mimosa? Or tea to start while you look over the menu?"

"Hot tea would be nice." Her voice was soft. Sensitive.

"I'll bring that right over." He raced off to the coffee station. Jesus, what the fuck was wrong with him? She was just a customer. Like everyone else in the room.

And too freaking young. If she were older than twenty-six, he'd be shocked. He was thirty-seven, which was too much of an age difference, especially for dating without strings.

"What are you doing?" Veronica asked.

"Helping out." He lifted the mug with hot water, carefully placing a lemon wedge and a tea bag on the saucer.

"You're seriously going to wait on the hot chick?"

"We're down a waitress and you're doing double duty right now." He smiled. "It's the least I can do." Not wanting to hear another word, he turned on his heel and returned to the young woman digging through her purse. "Here you go."

"Thanks." She set her bag on the free seat.

"Have you decided? Because if you haven't, I can make a few recommendations."

"Um, I noticed a sign in the window for a waitress-hostess. Has that position been filled yet?"

"Nope. We just started looking today."

"Would it be possible to get an application?"

"Sure thing," he said. "And would you like anything to eat? We make a mean breakfast sandwich and our French toast is to die for."

"I'll just have some oatmeal."

"Coming right up and I'll bring over that application too." He headed toward the kitchen and put in the order before snagging the paperwork at the hostess station where Veronica stood, giving him the side-eye. "What?" He glared.

"Getting pen and paper to get her contact information?"

"Aren't you funny," he said. "If you must know, she's applying for the open position." Butterflies danced in his stomach like an incessant schoolgirl. Not that he knew what that was like. But it drove him batshit crazy. Whoever this woman was, she was just a girl. No one special.

"It certainly would be nice not to interview many people."

"Yup." He leaned against the podium, sucking in a

deep breath. "Are you sure one will be enough to help you?"

"Andrea will be back in two weeks. You're hiring someone to take over for me when I go on maternity leave. When I come back, you're going to be overstaffed."

"You're not going to want to work sixty hours a week when this little one comes and I'm sure your husband isn't going to want you to either."

"That's true." She patted his shoulder. "I really do appreciate all that you and your brothers have done for me. This has been the best job I've ever had."

"You're invaluable to us." He smiled. "I better go drop this off and make my rounds. If this weather holds up, we'll be opening the patio in a week or two."

"I'll have Jack ensure the heaters are ready."

"You're the best, Veronica."

"Pretty soon, you'll be saying it to that woman over there." Veronica laughed.

"You're being ridiculous."

"And you're acting like a fifteen-year-old boy about to get his first kiss."

Janelle (Aura) Kodi left enough cash on the table to pay the bill and leave an acceptable tip. She stood and stared out the window. This place was perfect. Better than perfect. It was a dream. It was everything she could have hoped for in both location and atmosphere.

She had weathered the storm and found a safe port.

It was far enough away from her previous life and to her knowledge, Lake George had no affiliations to her father's church or anyone like it. There might be other polygamists, but not all people who practiced plural families married off their young daughters to old men.

This was the spot. This was what she'd been searching for all along. She'd felt it the second she pulled in.

She mustered up all her strength and made her way to the front of the restaurant. She handed the job application to the handsome man, Phoenix, at the hostess station. She wasn't sure she'd ever seen anyone so beautiful before. He had kind, soulful eyes. They reminded her of Jason, the man who saved her three years ago.

She owed Jason her life. Her freedom.

Yet there were parts of her that still felt trapped in the past. She still constantly looked over her shoulder, especially now with her father's church making headlines.

Another possible relocation for her siblings.

Her sister wives.

No. They weren't that anymore. She had left all that behind.

"I noticed you didn't put a home address down," Phoenix said. "We're going to need that."

"I'm sorry, but I haven't found a place to live yet. I just rolled into town and saw the sign for a waitress needed in the window when I stopped for breakfast." Janelle had done everything that Jason had told her to do. She paid for things in cash when she could. She moved every couple of months. She did her best to blend in. While she was friendly, she didn't make connections. It could be lonely at times, but it was better than living in Arizona at the compound in what she now knew was a cult led by her father.

However, it had been three years, and Jason had told her that with space and time, she could settle down in one spot and live her life without fear. Once out, they had no claim. They couldn't force her to return. They certainly weren't going to report her missing. That would expose them and the culture. By now, she should be a faded memory in their minds. She hadn't come forward, and she had no plans to, although she carried a fair amount of guilt for not doing so.

"I see your last employment was at a bar and restaurant in Buffalo. But you only worked there for four months. Before that, it was Cleveland. Same thing." He leaned against the podium. "Do you mind if I ask why?"

This was always one of the most challenging questions to answer. She never quite knew how to spin it. The longest she ever stayed anywhere had been five months. "To be honest, I've been looking for that perfect place to land after losing my family." Not a total lie. She had lost everything she thought at one point she held dear.

"I'm so sorry," Phoenix said. "If I were to consider hiring you, I'd need a commitment for longer than the summer rush."

"When I left Ohio, I had planned to make my way here. This has been where I wanted to be for a while now. I can make that promise. As long as I can find a place to live."

Phoenix glanced over his shoulder, rubbing his chin. "I might be able to solve that problem for you too."

"Excuse me?"

"Hang on." He stepped away from the hostess

station to the board by the front door. He pulled down a piece of paper and handed it to her.

She glanced over the words on the page.

"I happen to be the landlord," Phoenix said. "Since we do background checks here at the restaurant, I wouldn't need to do a second one to rent."

"Is it furnished?" Thankfully, her hands didn't tremble. She'd learned to control that fearful response about two years ago. But her heart thumped in the center of her throat. Her palms grew sweaty and she could feel the heat rise across her chest. Being frightened of her own shadow had become a way of life. She'd gotten better over the years at being alone, but she'd grown tired of it. She wanted to experience all that life had to offer.

Jason told her that one day, things would be normal.

But she had no idea what that even looked like. She could barely function in the real world.

Sure, she'd learned how to drive. She'd gotten a high school equivalency. Every single employer hated seeing her go. Her previous landlords all adored her and the last one was absolutely willing to give her a good recommendation as a renter. She'd managed to function without ever standing out.

"Scantly," he said.

"What does that mean, exactly?"

"It has a bed with a dresser. A sofa and television. Along with a two-person table with a functional kitchen. But that's about it."

"That's enough for one person," she said, staring at the price. "Is it available now and do you require first and last months' rent?"

"Yes, and yes. Would you be good with a one-year lease?"

"I want this job, so yeah. I would." This was it. After three years, she was finally going to start her new life.

"I need to—"

"Phoenix, I'm so sorry to interrupt." Veronica appeared at Phoenix's side, gripping his arm. "I just got a call from my husband. His dad had a stroke. I hate to do this to you, but I have to go. Now."

"Veronica, don't apologize. Go take care of your family. We'll be fine." He squeezed her shoulder. "Please call me later and give me an update, okay?"

"I will." Veronica nodded as she raced out the front door.

"I don't know why I thought she was your wife." Oh my. Janelle did not mean to say that out loud.

"That's the first time anyone has ever said that. We're more like brother and sister." He chuckled. "How do you feel about working the hostess station? Breakfast this time of year is slow. Lunch might get a little busy today, but we have a great system for seating and I can show you that. Our other hostess is coming in at four, so you can go after that. I'll start the paperwork for both employment and rental and if all goes well, the job and apartment can be yours."

"Thank you so much. I won't let you down." She glanced at her clothes. "But I don't think I'm dressed appropriately."

"I'll get you a Blue Moon shirt. Jeans are fine in this establishment. We're pretty relaxed unless we're doing an event," he said. "The only other thing I'll need from you is to fill out the official application for my rental, with references."

"Not a problem. I can also give you two other past employers to call if you'd like them."

He tapped the paper in his hands. "I think the ones you listed on this should be enough. I'll show you around and get you settled. I think you'll like it here."

"I've already fallen in love with the town, so I'm sure I'm going to really enjoy it." Now all she needed to do was find a way to stop staring at the man. In all her travels and working at diners, pit stops, truck stops, and even a few upscale restaurants, she'd never once found herself attracted to a man. The idea of being with someone made her skin crawl after her experience with her so-called spiritual husband.

"All right. Follow me. There's a break room next to the kitchen. We have lockers for our employees to put their stuff. I'll introduce you to the breakfast chef. She's amazing." He placed his hand on the small of her back.

Holding her breath, she did her best not to retreat. Human touch was still something she struggled with. Hopefully, he didn't notice.

2

Phoenix stared at the computer screen, tapping his pen against the desk. He read and reread the report. A million things went through his mind. None of them great. But they all landed in one area. He picked up his cell and texted both his brothers. While the rental didn't affect them, hiring Janelle did.

Nelson: *I just pulled into the parking lot. I'll be up in the office in five.*

Maverick: *In the kitchen. On my way.* The sound of the office door opening caught his attention. He glanced over his shoulder. "Hey, big brother. How's that baby girl of yours?"

"Keeping us up all night." Nelson plopped down on the small sofa on the other side of the room. "Sleeps great during the day but is up every few hours to eat, and then from three in the morning to about seven, she's ready to scream bloody murder."

Maverick strolled through the door. He sat on the armrest next to Nelson. "Mom said that's how Phoenix was, but worse. That little shit cried day and night and constantly woke the two of us up, making us all miserable."

"Dad told me the colic lasted over three months. Brandi's going to lose her shit if this lasts that long." Nelson rubbed his eyes. "It's crazy. She'll go from being so cute and sweet to being a soul-sucking devil."

"I can't wait to watch you navigate Lilly as a teenager and her bringing home a boy with tattoos," Phoenix said.

"Don't even put that out in the universe." Nelson raked his fingers through his unruly hair. "I met the new hire. Good on you for filling that position fast and with someone who seems incredibly competent. I watched her for a few moments when I walked in. She's friendly, though a little quiet, and greeted me immediately."

"Yeah. She's a fast learner and isn't afraid of hard work." Phoenix returned to the report his mom's friend sent over. "Only, I might have found something troubling."

"What's that?" Maverick asked.

"Since I'm considering renting her my garage apartment, I used Mom's contacts to do a rush background check and this is what came up." He tapped his finger on the screen. "I'm not sure what to make of it or how to handle it."

"You're seriously going to make me stand after the night I had?" Nelson leaned forward. "Just tell me what it says."

Phoenix tapped a few keystrokes. "At first glance, everything adds up. She looks great on paper. But you know Mom's contact. She always goes the extra mile, so she pulled a few more records no one would ever do on a regular background check."

"You're stalling," Maverick said. "Spill it."

"Basically, the name she gave me is for a person who died in 1922."

"Well, that is interesting." Maverick inched closer, examining the screen. "But nothing negative on the current identity? How long has it been active?"

"I didn't have them go back very far," Phoenix said. "And Mom's friend said it appears to be from a pool of identities used to help hide people."

"She didn't give me a criminal vibe," Nelson said calmly. One of the things he appreciated about his family was that they never jumped to conclusions, even when one appeared obvious. "Not that I've spent any time with her. What are your thoughts?"

"She's reserved and a bit on the shy side," Phoenix said. "I called her previous employers along with her last two known addresses. Everyone gave her glowing recommendations. Her employers told me she was a hard worker. Almost never called in sick. Was always on time. Stepped up when needed. Did more than what was required. Her landlords all reported she was only late on rent once or twice and always went to them ahead of time when she was struggling. She was clean. Never had parties and left the apartments better than when she arrived."

"Sounds like a model employee and an ideal renter," Nelson said.

"Or too good to be true." Maverick cocked a brow. "Have you been able to do a financial report?"

"I did some poking and the girl has almost no money. A small savings account, which will be nearly wiped out when she gives me three months of rent up front, but she's managed to keep a decent credit score by not going into debt. Nothing stands out as negative."

Nelson cocked his head. "You both have to be thinking the same thing I am."

"My brain went there," Maverick said.

"Oh, hell yeah. She flinched when I put my hand on her back to guide her to the break room. And I'm not talking like I startled her. I'm talking like she was freaked out because a man put his hands on her, but the chick's only twenty-six years old."

"Veronica's twenty-five and she's married and pregnant," Nelson said. "Abuse can happen to anyone at any time in their life and some people marry young." He pursed his lips. "You should know that better than anyone."

"I know." Phoenix let out a long breath. For the most part, he stayed out of people's personal lives. Everyone had baggage, including him. But there was one thing he couldn't tolerate.

A man raising his hand to a woman in anger.

When he'd been a teenager, the mother of one of his best friends had been beaten to death by his father. It had been the single most tragic thing that Phoenix had ever experienced. The truly hard part had been that people knew and no one did anything about it. Some tried. She even escaped once, but ultimately, she went back and she was killed a few short weeks later.

His friend, Max, had never been the same after that. He blamed himself for not protecting his mom. He'd only been fourteen. And his father had taken a baseball bat to him more than once.

Shortly after high school, Max took his own life.

It changed Phoenix on a fundamental level.

"The good news is someone helped her get a new

identity and did it right, based on what I'm looking at. A regular background check wouldn't have found out what we just did. Records that far back can be tricky." Phoenix spent his spare time volunteering at a women's shelter. Helping them escape their abusers gave him great pleasure. He'd been too young, and frankly, too scared, to help his friend. But he could pay it forward as an adult. "If I had gone the traditional route, all I would have learned was this person has no criminal background. No liens or judgments. There'd be no red flags for us not to hire her or for me not to rent her the apartment."

"So, what do you want to do?" Nelson sat up taller, stretching. "We could ask Mom's contact to dig deeper."

"We do that and we risk exposing her to whoever she's potentially running from. I know from experience that's not a good idea." Phoenix rose. He stared out the window that overlooked the bar area.

Janelle greeted a couple of customers and showed them to a table before helping bus an empty one. It was not something she needed to do as acting hostess, but going the extra mile was always something they looked for in their employees. "My gut tells me she's a woman starting her life over and doesn't need us sticking our noses where they don't belong." In the last year, he'd put two young mothers up in a hotel so they would have a safe place while the police sorted out their situation. The system didn't work fast enough and often didn't help these women in the real ways they needed. But he did what he could. "The records I do have only date back fifteen months. If someone is looking for her, like a dick abusive husband, she's not safe and it could put her in a dangerous situation if we dig too deep."

"I don't want you to get pissed at me for saying this, but we're speculating and that can put us between a rock and a hard place if we're wrong," Nelson said.

"I don't think we are." Phoenix turned to face his brothers. "I looked into her eyes and there's a world of hurt there. I've seen it before. I know what that looks like, and while she might be a few miles down the road, it's still there."

"But you don't know what or who put it there." Nelson rubbed the back of his neck. "You don't have to rent her the apartment."

"No. I've already decided to do that. I'm not going to turn her away. Not unless you or Maverick have any real concerns you want to share with me," Phoenix said.

"I get this subject is a touchy one for you." Maverick rested his hand on Phoenix's shoulder. "I'm behind your decision, whatever it is."

"I trust your gut on this one." Nelson jumped to his feet. "If I don't get some caffeine in me, I'm going to fall asleep."

"Why don't you go home?" Phoenix lowered his chin.

"Agreed," Maverick said. "I don't know what that newborn stage is like, but I do know what it's like to have kids that don't sleep. That was us the first month we adopted Ashley and Cole."

"You two have been doing so much lately. I feel like I'm letting you down."

Phoenix shook his head. "Eventually, that little princess of yours will sleep through the night and you'll be able to do more. I'm not stressed over it."

"Neither am I," Maverick said. "I'm sure Hensley won't care if I work late tonight."

"I'll take the morning shift." Nelson held up his hand. "I insist. Lilly's up anyway. That way you two can sleep in and deal with the nights."

"Works for me." Phoenix nodded.

"When are you letting Janelle move in?" Maverick asked.

"I'm going to tell her she can have it starting today if she wants it. But that's entirely up to her." Phoenix glanced over his shoulder. The lunch crowd had dwindled down to a few tables. A few of the waitresses had already clocked out and the rest were busy cleaning tables and preparing for the early birds. It would be light, but it would be busier than last week.

"Well, I'm going to get the hell out of here before one of you change your mind," Nelson said.

"I'll check in later." Phoenix gave his brother a manly hug.

"Give Janelle our numbers in case she needs anything. And you better warn Mom and Dad you rented the place to a young woman who doesn't need Mom to play matchmaker with because you know she will." Nelson pulled open the door and jogged down the steps.

"It's going to be a fine line with what I tell Mom." If Phoenix told his mom exactly what he was thinking, she'd be over every day to check in with Janelle. If he told her nothing, she'd be doing her damndest to make them a couple. But being vague could be worse because then his mom might believe he was keeping secrets and that didn't go over well in his family.

"She's so busy being a grandma and trying to help Hensley at the office, so she might stay out of your business," Maverick said.

"That's the funniest thing I've heard in a long time," Phoenix said. "I'm going to go downstairs and see how Janelle is doing."

"All right. I'm going to go through the morning receipts. I'll chat with you later."

Phoenix made his way down the stairs. He leaned against the bar and watched as Janelle hustled to help the waitresses and busboys get ready for the next crowd. He understood her job today was to impress her new boss. Make a good impression with the rest of the staff and do a good job for the customers.

She hit all three and then some.

While she carried herself with a sense that she could do any task, she didn't exude confidence. She did look people in the eye, but she didn't always hold that stare. Her gaze dropped to the floor or shifted somewhere else. During the initial rush, she got flustered once and one of the waitresses got short with her. Janelle immediately became quiet and apologetic for something she had no control over.

"Need anything, boss?" Jack, the bartender and one of their managers, asked.

"I'm good, thanks," Phoenix said. "What do you think of the new girl?"

"She's good. If I'm busy, she doesn't mind coming back here and getting water, soda, drinks, whatever she needs. I can see one or two of the other girls getting a little pissy about Janelle taking the initiative, but we know who they are."

"Yeah, we do. And one of them is on thin ice."

Phoenix and his brothers were close to firing one of the girls. A discussion they had yet to have. They'd had a couple of employees leave for various reasons, but they had yet to have to fire anyone. Perhaps Janelle was exactly what Pamela needed. "Maybe this will give Pam an incentive to do better."

"Or be more of a bitch," Jack said. "Sorry, boss. But you're missing one key element when it comes to Pam. She's crushing on you hard."

"That hasn't gone over my head. Trust me. And now she's texting me privately. Something I need to deal with." Phoenix cringed as Pam sashayed across the bar area, waving with a smirky smile that he wondered if it was supposed to be sexy. "But for now, I choose to ignore it."

Pam had been around for a while. When she first started at Blue Moon, she'd been a decent waitress. Not great, but she got the job done. He hadn't seen how badly she wanted to date him, which was never going to happen.

Not because she wasn't attractive, because she was quite pretty. But looks didn't mean much. She could be kind. She was good to the customers, which mattered. However, she was highly competitive and not always in a good way when it came to the other waiters and waitresses. She spoke too much about herself in a bragging fashion. She tended to be tone deaf in conversations, making them about herself and not the topic at hand.

Phoenix did his best to keep his distance both at work and in town. However, she managed to be at every turn. She was there if he went out with a buddy for a beer somewhere else. She strolled in with her friends if he hung late at Blue Moon when it wasn't his turn to work. And she was always flirting with him, dropping hints on where she lived and what she'd be doing the next day.

It was gross and kind of pathetic.

"How's that working for ya, boss?" Jack chuckled. "Because the more you avoid telling her that she's delusional, the more she's going to keep giving you that look and telling the rest of us it's just a matter of time before she's shedding the apron and being the boss' wife."

Phoenix dropped his chin to his chest and groaned. "Please tell me she's not saying that to other employees."

"Oh, she has," Jack said. "And look, here she comes all smiley and weird."

"Wonderful," Phoenix mumbled.

"Hi, Phoenix. How are you today?" Pam leaned against the counter, smiling wide and pushing her chest out.

"I'm good. Looks like we had a decent breakfast and lunch crowd," he said.

"Things are picking up, that's for sure." She glanced over her shoulder. "I was surprised you hired someone so quickly. I don't mean to question your judgment or anything, but she seems a little green. I've been helping her out and I'm sure she'll get it. But I thought you would have interviewed a few more girls." She tilted her head. "Like a friend of mine that I told about the position who was going to come in this afternoon."

"I'm sorry about your friend." Phoenix wanted to burst out laughing over some of Pam's comments. They were beyond comical, especially regarding Janelle's work ethic. "I hadn't realized you'd recommended someone for the position. However, it's been filled. If something comes up again, I'll let you know and give that person first opportunity."

"I appreciate that." She rested her elbows on the bar, which only accentuated her breasts. "Do you have big plans tomorrow night?"

"I'll be working."

"I'm having a small gathering at my place. I'd love it if you could make it."

"It's not a good time for me."

"How about another night?" she asked. "We could go out for drinks and maybe a movie or something."

Jack let out a slight snicker, followed by a cough, and then he pounded his chest and cleared his throat. With more gusto than necessary, he cleaned the countertop.

"Let's step outside for a second." Phoenix pointed toward the outdoor patio. He stuffed his hands in his pockets because no way was he going to do the gentlemanly thing and guide her through the room. He did, however, open the door when he got there. It wasn't the first time that Pam had asked him to go out, but this had to be the last.

"It's so pretty out here." She gripped the railing. "One of these days I'm going to live on the lake. It's so picturesque." She turned. "I bet you get amazing sunsets at your place."

He wasn't about to entertain that conversation. "I asked you out here because I need to make something perfectly clear and I didn't want to do it in front of an audience."

"I totally understand. Nothing worse than workplace gossip." She took a step closer, resting her hand on his biceps.

Jesus. Was this chick for real? "No. I don't think you get it." He moved back, raking his fingers through his hair. "I don't want to make this awkward or uncomfortable for you. However, I need you to stop flirting and asking me out. I'm your boss. I don't date my employees. And for the record, I wouldn't be interested even if you didn't work here. I'm sorry if that seems harsh. You're a nice person, but we don't have a connection."

She narrowed her stare and folded her arms across her chest. "How would you know if we've never seen each other outside of Blue Moon?" She reached for his arm again. "One date. How could it hurt?"

He jerked his arm. "Pam, I'm not going to say this again. You have to stop this, especially at work."

"I get it. You're worried about what everyone else will say. We can keep it out of the workplace. No one will have to know. At least not right now."

"No. That's not what I'm saying." He did his best to rein in his frustration. The woman didn't listen. "Nothing is ever going to happen. We're never going to go out. Ever. We need to keep things strictly professional. Now, let's get back to work." He waved his arm toward the door.

"At work, I can do that." She held her head high and strolled back into the restaurant, swaying her hips.

"Good Lord," Phoenix muttered. He waited a good three minutes before he followed, making his way behind the bar.

"She's still smiling. I'm not sure you're getting

through to her," Jack said. "As a matter of fact, she looks like she's glowing."

"That's not funny." Two tables in the main dining room were occupied and one person sat at the end of the bar; otherwise, the place was dead. Then again, it was half past three. In about twenty minutes, the early bird group would show up and the rest of the night should be a steady flow of customers.

The beginning of a new season always brought a sense of excitement. Blue Moon had become one of the most talked about restaurants in the area. They were known for good food, great music, and an even better ambiance. He and his brothers had done exactly what they had set out to do, and they made a nice profit doing it.

So why did he feel as though his life wasn't where he wanted it to be? It was a question that had plagued him for the last few months.

Janelle strolled in his direction. She'd picked up a waitress apron and had been cleaning tables and setting them up for the dinner rush.

"What do you think of Blue Moon so far?" he asked.

"I love it." She smiled. "I've met both your brothers. They seem cool and very helpful."

"I should warn you that they live on my street and always show up unannounced."

Her eyes went wide.

"Oh, don't worry. They won't go near the apartment. But you will see them in and out of the main house. Along with their wives and children."

"How many kids do they have?"

"Maverick has two. Ashley is three and Cole is a year and a half. Nelson has a newborn little girl named Lilly."

She pulled the rental agreement from the apron. "I had a chance to review this on my break and I wanted to ask you an awkward and uncomfortable question."

"All right."

"How many hours can you give me? Because I'm a little worried about the rent based on the hourly wage."

"Shit. I must have given you the summer lease and not the yearlong one." He took it from her hands and scanned the short document. Total lie, but he didn't give a shit. "Yep. So sorry. I had two different monthly prices depending on what kind of rental I got. Summer leases are insane here and I could probably get double that if I tried. So, we can knock five hundred off the rent."

"Are you sure?" She jerked her head. "That's a lot of money."

"Positive." He snagged a pen and scribbled the

new price. "As far as hours go, I'll do my best to schedule you a full forty a week. But until Veronica goes on maternity leave, I can't guarantee it." He held up his hand. "But if you're willing to bus tables, wash dishes, or whatever, I can call you when someone phones in sick or we're short for whatever reason."

"Hey, boss," Jack said. "I didn't mean to eavesdrop, but don't forget, Larry's taking two weeks off soon and I could use the help behind the bar. Does the new girl know anything about bartending?"

"I know some," Janelle said. "But I'm a quick study."

"Works for me if you don't mind a little overtime to stand behind the bar with Jack." Phoenix handed her the rental agreement back.

"I don't mind one bit. I don't like sitting on my butt doing nothing." She smiled.

It damn near knocked Phoenix on his ass. "Why don't you go take a quick break and grab something to eat."

"Thanks. I'm starving." She raced off toward the kitchen.

"Now I don't have to work with Pam." Jake patted himself on the shoulder.

"At least I hadn't promised her those hours, but she's going to flip when I make my brothers tell her that the new girl's getting them," Phoenix said.

"She's already fuming." Jack laughed. "Because, dude, you're smitten."

"Smitten? What the fuck does that even mean?" Phoenix held up his hand. "Don't bother. I don't want to hear it." He glanced at his watch. "I think I'm going to go grab some grub."

Jack let out a full-on belly laugh.

Phoenix ignored him and made his way to the kitchen. Time to get to know Janelle a little bit better.

3

Janelle stood on the porch of her apartment and stared at the sunset. In all her travels she'd seen many, but none affected her as deeply as this one. The sun dipped behind the mountaintops, leaving behind an array of colors. Orange. Purple. Red. They all streaked across the sky like a wild painting taking shape. It took her breath away.

It not only represented her freedom, but it gave way to a fresh beginning. She'd driven through the storm and perhaps found home.

The sound of an engine rumbling down the road filled her ears. She turned.

Phoenix's truck pulled into the driveway. He waved as the garage door lifted.

His home was nothing she'd ever seen before. It

was magical, like the lake it overlooked. She'd been inside the main house once during the week she'd lived inside the detached garage apartment, and she'd honestly been shocked at the size of his home along with his beautiful decor. All the furnishings were a combination of white and blue leather. The kitchen was white and gray with this swirly countertop that had a waterfall island in the middle. A big picture window in the family room gave way to the most spectacular view of the crisp waters below.

And he hadn't skimped on the apartment. When he told her it had been scantly furnished, she'd been prepared for what she'd rented in the past. Most of her previous places had sagging beds with sofas that matched. But this place had a big queen-sized bed that had to be brand new. It had a whitewashed wood headboard with a matching dresser. There was a place for her to sit at the foot of the bed. The couch was a light-green leather and it was soft, plush, and super comfortable. She felt like a princess in a castle.

"Hey, you," he called from the driveway. "Have you had dinner yet?" he asked, holding up a bag.

"Um, well, no." Lying, while she'd gotten good at it when it came to her past, wasn't something she liked to do when it came to her everyday life. She wanted to be as authentic as she could be in this new world she was trying to create.

"Are you hungry? Because I've got enough here for two."

"Aren't you supposed to be working the dinner crowd?" Thus far, she'd worked every day this week, including this morning and through the lunch shift. Tomorrow she was scheduled for dinner to close and then a much-needed day off.

Although, she didn't actually require it, but Phoenix and his brothers did, so she'd act as though she would enjoy the rest.

"Lilly actually slept all night and had a decent day today, so Nelson wants to work. I'm not going to argue with him, especially when I'm dead dog tired and could use a break."

Janelle loved watching the Snow brothers and their interactions with each other. It's what she remembered from her early years, before her father got weird and twisted the doctrine of his church. If she were being honest with herself, perhaps her dad's vision had always been there, but her biological mother and her grandfather, an elder in the church, kept her dad in check.

Once her grandpa and mother passed, everything changed.

And not for the better.

Her stomach growled. While the tips at Blue Moon were good, she'd yet to receive her first full paycheck and her savings had been depleted after giving Phoenix first, last, and a security deposit. That meant she had to be frugal and she was living on noodles and toast with a few strawberries and salad as a treat. Of course, peanut butter and jelly too.

"I wouldn't want to impose on your time off. I know how hard you work." She also wasn't sure being alone with a man who stirred emotions in her that she'd never felt before nor knew how to deal with was a good idea. Working with him was one thing, but she had no idea how to behave with anyone on an individual basis.

"Trust me, you're not. Besides, I don't want to eat alone. I called my parents, but they're on a date night and Maverick is up to his eyeballs with his two little ones and bath time. So, if you don't have big plans, come and join me. I snagged some steaks from the restaurant. I have potatoes, green beans, and a nice bottle of red. I'm good with a grill." He smiled wide. "I'm not going to take no for an answer."

Her heart thumped heavily in the center of her chest. Saying no would only insult her boss, something she didn't want to do. "All right."

"Cool. Come on down. The front door's open."

"But." She waved a finger. "I'm not the biggest fan of beans, so I'll bring a salad."

"Fair enough." He nodded. "Let yourself in."

"See you in a couple of minutes."

He turned and disappeared back into his garage. The door rattled, closing behind him.

Sighing, she made her way back inside with her muscles shaking like a volcano. Men had asked her out before and she'd always said no. She wasn't comfortable being alone with members of the opposite sex. Her life experiences had been limited to the world in which she'd grown up. Her marriage had been a prison. It had been abusive both physically and sexually. She hadn't really understood, except deep down she knew what was happening to her wasn't right. That God didn't want this for any woman.

However, it had taken the loss of a child for Janelle to find the courage to leave.

She opened the fridge and found the pre-made salad she'd splurged on with this morning's tips. The one thing she'd learned from the last three years was that what you put out in this universe, you got back. She smiled at every customer. No matter how uncomfortable it made her feel, she made eye contact. She hustled her ass to ensure that every person who walked into Blue Moon believed she was there to serve them and did her best to give them the service they desired.

So far, it had paid off.

Only, at every turn, it pissed off one person.

Pam. That woman did not like Janelle and Janelle couldn't figure out why.

Jack kept telling her not to worry about Pam. That eventually, Pam would soften; she always did.

But Janelle wasn't so sure. Pam reminded her of Tracy, one of her sister wives. Tracy had a need to be Jim's favorite and did whatever she had to in order to ensure she was always in his favor. Even if that meant calling out all the other sister wives, instead of supporting them.

A covenant of their religion.

Janelle put the salad in a bowl and headed for the main house with her pulse in her throat.

The last time she'd been alone with a man had been after she ran away.. Jason had been so kind and caring. He gave her space. He never once touched her, as if he understood her aversion to human contact. But Jason had grown up in a cult. He had working knowledge of what it was like to be Janelle.

She scurried down the outside stairs. The fact that Phoenix had made two entrances so that during the winter months, she wouldn't have to deal with the elements and could also park her car in the detached garage said something about the man's character.

At least that's what she'd like to believe.

When she left her father's church, she lacked a

basic understanding of how the outside world worked. She was raised to believe that the government, law enforcement, and anyone who wasn't inside the compound walls were evil.

She now knew that wasn't true, but that still didn't alleviate her trust issues with people in general.

Holding the salad bowl in one hand, she tapped on the door before pushing it open. "Phoenix?"

"In the kitchen. Come on in."

As she strolled through the living room, she paused at the fireplace to look at all the family pictures. Him with his brothers in their military uniforms. Him with his parents and brothers. Him with his nieces and nephew. Him with his parents. It was apparent that this man was a family man.

She wasn't sure if that made this harder.

Or easier.

"Thanks for inviting me." She set the bowl on the island.

The steaks were on a platter. He lifted a cookie sheet of potatoes and placed them in the oven. "I'll be honest, I brought home two hoping you'd be around." He took the bottle of wine and poured two glasses, handing her one.

Drinking had been against the church. It was the devil's juice, and if you partook, you were going to hell. Since she left, she found herself enjoying a few sips here and there, but she never bought it and brought it into her home. Some habits were hard to break.

"Thank you." She raised the glass to her lips and took a tiny sip. Her taste buds went wild. It wasn't too sweet. Had a dry, rich flavor to it. And it went down smoothly. She took a larger sip, enjoying the way it hit her belly. "This is really good."

"My brothers and I went to this little town in New Jersey called Candlewood Falls. There's a winery there that we fell in love with. The River Winery. They have some great blends. We've gotten to know the owners because we served with one of their sons, Corbin River. Anyway, we buy it by the case now."

"That's nice you can support your friend's family," she said. "Can I help with anything?"

"Nope." He smiled that wicked grin of his. It made his blue eyes twinkle. "The potatoes will take about forty minutes and the steaks need to rest. It will be a good twenty minutes or so before I can start grilling, so why don't we go sit outside on the deck and enjoy this awesome evening. The temperatures have really turned. I think we'll have an early start to summer, which will mean a busy season for Blue Moon."

"I've noticed that you have a lot of regulars."

He placed his hand on the small of her back.

Every muscle in her body tensed. She blinked, wishing she could control that knee-jerk response.

He removed his hand, pulling back the sliders, but said nothing of her reaction.

"You're so lucky to live here," she whispered. "I have to pinch myself that I stumbled upon this rental."

"My mom is constantly telling us boys that everything happens for a reason, which is funny because Mom can be such a cynic."

"Really? I've met your mom. She's so positive and upbeat." She took a seat in one of the big Adirondack chairs.

"That she is." He laughed. "But she's also retired CIA and has seen some shit in her day. My dad was a general in the Army and he's pretty hardened too. So the fact that they are both so warm and fuzzy these days cracks the three of us up."

Her heart skipped a beat. FBI, CIA, and DEA were all three letters she'd learned to loathe and mistrust. They were the organizations that wanted to separate women from their children and put men in jail.

The last part she knew needed to be done.

But the former she still didn't agree with. They were innocents in a world that predators had created.

Quickly, she pushed those thoughts out of her

mind. No one here wanted to hurt her or take her away. She'd done nothing wrong.

Except not speak up.

But as Jason had explained, she needed to save herself.

She watched how Phoenix held his wineglass by the stem, swirling the liquid before taking a sip. He was everything she wasn't.

Sophisticated and worldly.

"Your parents had interesting jobs," she said, trying to carry on with the conversation. "What did you do before Blue Moon?"

"My brothers and I were in the Army. Special Forces."

Shit. She knew that. "That's a dangerous job," she managed.

"I can't deny that," he said, leaning against the railing. "I was injured on a mission that took me off active duty. I was headed for a desk job when my brothers left the military. We had always said when I hit twenty years, since I'm the youngest, we'd all open a business together. That just happened a few years before we planned."

Fascinated by this man and his family's history, she leaned forward. "Why did your brothers leave?"

"Nelson left because of a mission that had gone sideways, basically ruining his career. Maverick had left before him for a woman. But she turned out to be a mistake. We all came up here where Nelson found Brandi and Maverick found Hensley." Phoenix smiled. "My parents joined us, which is nice that the whole family is now in one place."

"What about you? Anyone special in your life?" Holy crap. Did she ask him that question? It was too personal and that was something she didn't want to get into, but she found herself wanting to know everything about this man. It was an unwelcome sensation that she had no control over.

He chuckled. "Nope."

"I find that hard to believe."

"Believe it." He took a long sip of his beverage. "I've never been the settling down type of guy like my brothers who have wanted marriage and kids."

"You don't want that?"

He shifted, turning his gaze toward the horizon. "I can't say that I have. My folks believe it's because of the girls I tend to date. My brothers think I'm afraid of commitment."

"What do you believe?" She needed to stop asking questions. This wasn't like her at all. She was the kind of woman who didn't speak unless spoken to. That was something she carried from her past. She didn't get close to people because she was never going to stay anywhere too long and even though she planned on staying in this place longer, she still needed to keep a safe distance.

"That's a good question and one that I have no answer for anymore." He pushed from the railing and eased into the chair next to her. "For years it was because I didn't have time. I was focused on my career in the Army. I was deployed so much it wouldn't be fair to anyone I was with. My mom said that was an excuse because she and my dad always made it work, which is true. I had a great childhood even though my dad was gone a lot and my mom's job was demanding as hell."

"Can I ask you a question?"

He burst out laughing. "That's all you've been doing, but sure. Go ahead."

She took a sip of courage. "Did you join the Army because that's what you were expected to do?"

"God, no," he said. "My parents discouraged it to a point. They didn't want us boys to sign up because it was the only life we knew. But I have no regrets. I loved my career. Working with my dad and brothers and even my mom on some missions. It was a great life. I'd do it all over again if given the opportunity."

She wished she could say the same.

The only thing she would repeat was leaving.

He lifted his chair, turning it to face her. "What

about you? This might be a big assumption on my part, but I take it you're single."

"Very much so," she said with a nervous laugh.

"Do you want to get married someday? Have kids?"

A flash of her past filled her brain. It was one of the most painful memories of her life. At the time, she thought having a baby would give her something to connect with. Something to love. Someone to give her purpose in a world that no longer made sense.

But that baby had never cried and both her husband and father had told her that child's death had been God's punishment.

She swallowed. Hard. "I don't know."

"Nothing wrong with that." He tapped his glass against hers. "So many people are hyper-focused on doing what they believe they're supposed to do instead of figuring out what they really want. I've been envious of my brothers for knowing they've always wanted a family. The only thing I've ever always known I wanted is to be close to Maverick and Nelson. They and my parents mean everything to me. I've got that. But now I find myself at a crossroads. Maybe it's my age. Maybe it's maturity. Or maybe it's finally being settled in one place. I have no idea. However, I do know I'm selfish. I like my space. I don't mind living alone. I'm just starting to feel like there might be more. Like something is missing." He shook his head. "This conversation went deep."

"I'm sorry. I didn't mean to pry."

He patted her forearm. "No. It's okay. It's nice. I don't normally talk about stuff like this. Not even to my brothers all that much these days, especially because they are always offering to set me up on dates and after my last couple experiences, I'm happy to sit back and let life happen on its terms." He leaned to the side and pulled out his cell. He rolled his eyes and audibly groaned.

"What's the... never mind. Not my business."

"It's about to be." He stood. "Pam is at the door." He waved his cell phone. "This might get awkward."

"Why?"

"You're about to find out."

This was getting fucking ridiculous.

Phoenix stomped through the living room. Ever since he'd told Pam there was no chance and to keep things strictly professional, she'd done the complete opposite. She wasn't too bad at work, but she would stop in the office and drop hints at when she would be alone at her place. Or ask when his next night off would be. She'd always be hush-hush about it, as if that was what he wanted.

And then the text messages.

Those were the worst.

He responded a couple of times, asking her not to text him because it was inappropriate.

She took that as she should call.

He didn't answer.

Sucking in a deep breath, he gripped the handle and yanked open the door. "Pam, what are you doing here? This is my home and I don't like it when people come over unannounced."

"You're joking, right?" She planted a hand on her hip, jutting it out. "You left work with two steaks. I heard you tell Jack you were hoping to cook dinner for someone. I was standing right there and you know I wasn't on the schedule for the evening shift."

"If I wanted to have you over, I would have asked." He raked his fingers through his hair. "I'm sorry, but I'm in the middle of something. Please don't come over again. I hate being rude, but you leave me with no other alternative." He was going to have to bring his brothers into the conversation. This bordered on harassment and he wasn't having anything to do with it.

Her big smile quickly faded. "What changed between when you left..." She peered over his shoulder. "...what is Janelle doing here?" Pam pushed him aside, nudging her way into his home.

"Pam. I have to ask you to leave." He held the door open, but she didn't listen. Fuck. This wasn't going to turn out well. "Seriously. What the hell do you think you're doing?"

As Pam stormed into the room, Janelle stood in the kitchen like a deer in headlights.

Phoenix raced through the living room. This was the last thing he needed. He was sure Janelle didn't need a confrontation with a co-worker.

"What's going on here?" Pam set her purse on the counter. She glanced between Phoenix and Janelle.

"Dinner, what does it look like?" Phoenix said with a long breath. "This is who I was planning on cooking for."

Pam's face hardened. "You've got to be kidding me. Next, you'll tell me she's the one who rented the garage apartment when I told you that I was interested in it."

Phoenix snagged the wine bottle and poured himself a large glass. "Only after I rented it and you have a place in town twice the size," he mumbled before chugging his wine, wishing it were a shot of tequila. "Pam, I'm going to walk you to your car so I can make things perfectly clear once and for all."

"Oh please, make them clear right here. I'm sure

Janelle would like to know about how you've been dating me—"

"For fuck's sake, Pam. We've never dated. We're never going to date. And if this doesn't stop, you're going to force my hand to take the kind of measure that won't be good for you." He pointed to the front door. "Please leave. Don't make me do this the hard way."

"Are you threatening me?" Pam glared.

"Take it however you want. But you are not welcome in my home. You're my employee. Nothing more. Nothing less."

"That's what Janelle is." Pam snagged her purse, aggressively putting it over her shoulder. She leaned closer to Janelle. "You're the new girl. I get it. All shiny and pretty. But remember, what he just did to me, he'll do to you." She looked Phoenix up and down. "I was warned about you. I didn't want to believe it, but everyone was right. You're a ladies' man. Just another notch in your bedpost." She turned on her heel and stormed through the house, slamming the front door.

Phoenix closed his eyes and counted to ten before opening them. "I'm sorry you had to witness that."

Janelle gripped the counter, saying nothing.

"Are you okay?" He rested his hand on her back, between her shoulder blades. Her breath came in short pants. He could feel her heart beat wildly out of control. "Hey. That had nothing to do with you. Pam has been hitting on me for weeks and I thought I had it handled. I've told her numerous times that I wasn't interested."

Janelle took in a slow breath. "I should go," she whispered.

"Don't let what happened ruin the nice time we've been having." He ran his hand up and down her tense back. He'd seen his share of battered women, and Janelle hit every single criterion.

She flinched every time he touched her.

She couldn't deal with confrontation.

She was soft-spoken and struggled with authority.

But this seemed over the top.

A jealous woman getting under her skin like that shouldn't be such a big trigger. Unless it was the way he handled it. He'd done his best to keep his voice level. He hadn't yelled. Sure, he swore, but he'd been as respectful to both women as he could.

"I don't want to cause problems with you and others at work," she said.

"Trust me, you're not." He took a chance and gently gripped her by the biceps, turning her to face him. He caught her gaze.

Tears filled her eyes. One dribbled down her cheek.

He wiped it away.

She inhaled sharply. "She's not going to be fun to work with."

"I will be having a conversation with my brothers. Whether you were here or not, her showing up at my house is grounds for dismissal. Not to mention she's been sending me texts that are borderline harassment. I'm going to be dealing with this. For now, I'll make sure you have minimal to no contact with her at work."

"I appreciate that." She swiped at her face. "I think we should call it a night."

"I'm disappointed because I was having a good time. But I can't make you stay."

"Thank you." She nodded. "I'll see you tomorrow."

He stood there and watched her leave. Whatever had happened to her in her past broke his fucking heart.

4

Janelle stood in front of her locker. The evening crowd had been a tad louder than expected due to the warmer temperatures, but the fat tips in her pocket were well worth the trouble.

Exhaustion settled into her bones. She hated to admit it, but she looked forward to doing absolutely nothing tomorrow.

"Is there anything you can't do?" Jack asked as he strolled into the break room. "I can't tell you how nice it is not to have to worry about stepping away from the bar when you're around."

"I'm glad you trust me," she said. "But I did screw up a few drinks."

"Don't stress about that. You did the right thing by asking the customer what was in it before trying to make the specialty beverage." He opened his locker and took out his leather jacket. "I've never seen anyone pick up our systems so fast before. Not that the way we do things is so complicated. But the Snow brothers can be quite demanding at times."

"I've worked for a lot worse than them," she said. "I find all three to be incredibly fair." She tugged at her bag and strapped it over her shoulder. Because someone had needed their shift covered, Pam had worked a few hours in the afternoon, making things incredibly awkward for Janelle.

And Phoenix.

Although, to Pam's credit, she stayed away from Janelle. But it was the cold shoulder that bothered Janelle. Pam had done her best to ignore Janelle to the point she wouldn't even help her when things got busy. Not that Janelle needed the aid, but it would have been nice considering Janelle bussed three of Pam's tables while she was on break.

It's what co-workers did regardless of their feelings for one another and Janelle was still confused as to what she'd done to Pam. Or what the real situation was regarding Pam and Phoenix. Janelle struggled to comprehend the dynamic. All she could equate it to was how Brother Jim had picked a favorite wife and Janelle was at the bottom of the barrel.

Phoenix had made his position clear; however,

he'd been harsh in his tone. The entire encounter was aggressive and that made Janelle more than uncomfortable.

"Mind if I give you a little unsolicited piece of advice?" Jack asked.

"Um, sure. Go ahead."

"I noticed some tension with you and Pam today. She almost always gives the new person a hard time. She likes to pawn off shit she doesn't like to do on others. You don't have to clear her tables all the time. She'll leave them for you because you did it once. She'll start bossing you around because she enjoys pulling the seniority card, but you're her equal. She's not above you. The only ones you have to listen to are Phoenix, his brothers, Veronica, and me."

"I'm here to work and if I see something that needs to be done, I'm not going to sit by and leave it."

"Just don't let anyone take advantage of you. Especially her." Jack glanced over his shoulder. "I probably shouldn't be saying anything, but she's got this weird idea that Phoenix is interested in her when he's not. He never has been and he never will be. He's tried to be nice, because that's who he is, but Pam has started to take it to a whole new level."

Janelle's pulse increased. This conversation was a little too intense. She wasn't used to being involved in other people's business. She wasn't sure what to say, much less how to act. She didn't understand her emotions. She'd never been jealous of her sister wives, even when they got Brother Jim's attention and she didn't. She never wanted her husband's affections, so if he spent all his nights with someone else, that was fine with her. The idea of becoming pregnant again had been horrifying. She couldn't go through that kind of pain again, and that was the only reason her husband would visit her at night.

She was the only sister wife who hadn't given him a child. She'd failed him, her father, and the church.

All she wanted to do was learn how to live in the real world. She wanted to put down roots. Have a job that put a roof over her head. Food on the table. Gas in her old beat-up car. And the ability to save a little so she could live out her days in peace.

Alone.

Making connections with people hadn't been part of the equation. But Jason had told her that when she found a place that sang to her soul, and her heart had begun to heal, it would be time to live. To find her people. She never thought that day would come.

But with each passing minute in Lake George, and at Blue Moon, she believed this could be the place.

However, the incident with Phoenix and Pam gave her pause.

"I also shouldn't say this, but I saw firsthand what Pam wants from Phoenix, and he wasn't very nice about letting her know that wasn't going to happen," she said. "But also, she made it sound like they had a thing."

Jack tossed his head back and laughed. "God, no. There is nothing there and Pam is full of shit. You know, she went after Maverick for a hot minute when she was first hired. Hensley put an end to that real quick when she came into the picture. The thing with Pam is she wants to marry a certain type of man. Phoenix checks all those boxes for her and then some." He leaned a little closer. "You're a threat to Pam."

She tapped the center of her chest. "Me? How?"

"Are you blind? Phoenix has been enamored with you since the moment you walked through that door. He's out in the main room waiting to walk you to your car."

"Excuse me?" She swallowed. Part of her was flattered. It reminded her of all the kind and sweet gestures that Jason had done three years ago. But Jason was married to Anne Marie. His affection stemmed from his passion to help girls like Janelle.

"I've known Phoenix since construction on this place began. He's a guarded man. The few women I've seen him date weren't the kind of ladies he could become attached to. He always told me he wasn't looking for anyone special. Just a good time and frankly, it showed. But in the past year, he's been restless. Barely taking anyone out. When you walked through that door, his eyes lit up like a damn Christmas tree."

"I'm not sure how to take that," she said softly.

Jack cocked his head. "He likes you. He's protective of you. I've never seen him like this before. Pam's noticed it and so have others. But she's the only one who has a problem with it because she's jealous. Not just because he likes you. Pays attention to you. But because you work your ass off and that's going to get you the extra hours when Veronica goes on maternity leave, and possibly her role as manager, something that Pam desperately wants but doesn't have the mindset for. Her actions today proved it to me and the Snow brothers."

"I don't want to come in here and upset the balance. She's been here longer. She deserves it."

"My God. You are a breath of fresh air." He patted her shoulder. "That attitude is why you'll end up getting it." He smiled. "I best get going. Enjoy your day off tomorrow." He turned and disappeared out the door.

She hugged her purse. That was a lot to take in. Part of her swelled with pride. The accolades felt good. During her time with Brother Jim, they were few and far between. These last three years, she'd kept her head down and did what she needed to in order to survive. She never stirred the pot. This was the first time that she had to deal with any real conflict and that made her want to run.

Again.

Something she'd become quite used to.

She sucked in a deep breath and headed into the bar area.

Phoenix leaned against the bar. "Hey, you," he said. "Ready to go home?"

"You didn't have to wait for me."

"Actually, I did." He held up a set of keys. "I have to lock up. Besides, while this is a safe area, I can't let you go out into the night alone. One never knows and my mother would have my head if I let a young woman walk to her car at night alone."

Back at the compound, women were only allowed to move about with their husband or father's permission. They could never leave the compound without a chaperone. They weren't allowed to talk to anyone in the outside world. Had Janelle not had so many complications with the stillbirth and had to be taken to the hospital, she would have never met Anne Marie.

She owed that woman her life.

Phoenix's gesture felt both comforting and confining at the same time. She appreciated his concern for her safety but resented how controlling it felt.

"Thank you." She knew enough about the outside world to comprehend that this should be considered an act of chivalry and she should be grateful.

"Come on." He waved his hand. "I'll follow you home."

Clutching her bag, she made her way out the door and toward the back parking lot where all the employees parked. There were only two vehicles left. Her dilapidated junker and his shiny pickup truck. Inwardly, she groaned.

"Well, shit," he said. "You have a flat tire."

"What?" She ran to her car and examined the rear driver's side tire, letting out an audible sigh.

"Not a big deal. I can change it for you."

"I don't have a spare," she said softly.

"Seriously?" He bent over, running his fingers over her tire. "Why not?"

"Because I got a flat a few months ago, and that is my spare."

He stood, raking his fingers through his thick, dark hair. "Why haven't you bought a new one?"

"I didn't have the funds at the time and I just haven't gotten around to it." She had to admit he was the most gorgeous man she'd ever met, and she had never looked at men. Ever. Not once did she ever consider dating. Jason told her that one day she would be able to have all the things that *normal* people had. A life filled with love and happiness.

If she wanted it.

But her only experience with what that looked like was a few couples she met along the way and Anne Marie and Jason.

They were an adorable couple. They held hands. Gazed into each other's eyes. Jason would kiss Anne Marie's temple. He would hold doors open for her and he treated her with respect.

Anne Marie did the same for him.

And Janelle never saw them yell at one another. She did see them argue, but she couldn't describe it as a fight. More like a disagreement that ended with them hugging. It was strange at times for Janelle to watch because she didn't understand. Anne Marie wasn't obedient. Or submissive. She was her own woman with her own thoughts and Jason valued them.

"Well, it's too late to do anything about it now," Phoenix said. "I'll drive you home. In the morning, I'll have it towed to a friend of mine who can replace the tire at a fair price. If you're that low on funds, I can advance you some money against your paycheck."

"Thank you for not offering to pay for it."

"I wouldn't dream of it." He laughed. "When my dad first started dating my mom, he made the mistake of offering to do something similar. My mother told him to take a leap off a bridge and almost didn't go out with him again."

"I really like your mother. She makes me laugh."

"Just don't get her going on stories about me and my brothers when we were little."

"Oh, now I'm going to have to ask." She found herself taking Phoenix's hand as he helped her into his massive truck. It was higher than normal and she needed to use the step to get in. But the really weird part was the electric shock that crawled across her skin from his touch. It ignited a flame in her belly. All her muscles tingled. She remembered Anne Marie telling her about the first time Jason kissed her and how magical it had been.

He likes you.

What exactly did that mean? And why did she

want it to be like all the romantic movies she'd watched on television?

It was as if she'd stepped out of her body and was watching someone else experience all these new sensations.

"Please don't," he said. "She likes to start off with the most embarrassing ones."

The truck roared to life. He pulled out onto the main road. The streets were dark and windy as they made their way toward home.

"I don't know what you were planning on doing on your day off, but if you need a car, you can borrow my truck. I have a second car I can drive."

"I've never driven anything this big. I don't think I could handle it."

"I'm sure you'll be fine, but if you know how to drive a stick, you can take the other one."

"I saw that fancy thing in your garage. No, thank you."

He laughed. "I just bought it. Picked it up three weeks ago. I've only had it out a couple of times."

"All the more reason I shouldn't be behind the wheel. Besides, I don't know how to drive a stick shift."

"You should learn," he said. "It's fun. I'm working in the morning but will be done after lunch. I can take you for a drive in it. I bet you haven't been able to see much of the town."

She stared out the window into the darkness. She wanted to go so desperately. She felt safe in his presence. Enjoyed his company more than anyone she'd met in a long while, but she was so confused by the way every fiber of her being responded to his voice. And now his touch.

She found herself wanting to know what it might be like to feel his lips pressed against hers, if only for a few seconds.

The world she'd come from had made her a wife at seventeen. Pregnant at eighteen. She'd miscarried numerous times and had a stillbirth, making her a failure at the one thing she had been put on this earth to achieve. Technically, she was an experienced woman, and yet she had no experience at all.

"I'd like that," she said.

"Good." He rolled to a stop in front of the detached garage next to his home. "Before you go up to bed, I do want to mention something to you."

"What's that?" She turned, holding his gaze, which sucked the air right out of her lungs.

"I'm sure you noticed that Veronica had to leave early today."

"I did," she said.

"She's having some difficulties with her pregnancy. Her doctor doesn't want her on her feet anymore."

"Oh no. That's terrible. I hope she and the baby are going to be okay." Instinctively, she placed her hand on her stomach.

"From what she told me, she's showing signs of early labor. She needs bed rest and that's what she's going to get. But she's a front manager and one of our best employees. I'm going to be having a meeting with my brothers and Jack first thing in the morning about how to deal with that and I'd like to toss your name out there for the position." He held up his hand. "It's temporary, until she comes back. It would mean a bump in pay and regular daytime hours, though we'd still need some swing shifts from you. But I wanted to ask you how you felt before I pushed that agenda."

"What about Pam? Or other people who have been there longer?"

He jerked his head. "I'm surprised Pam's name came out of your mouth, considering the way she has treated you, especially today. But she's not in the running, for more reasons than one. As far as everyone else goes, there will be others we discuss and you might not get it, so you need to be prepared for that."

"I don't know. I don't want to be the new girl whom no one likes."

"You work harder than anyone in Blue Moon outside of Jack. There's only one other person I would consider, and the only reason I wouldn't give it to them is because they prefer nights over days, and we need someone who can be on all days. You seem willing to work whatever hours we throw your way."

"I could certainly use the money." She gripped the door handle. "As long as you don't think it would cause too much of a disruption."

"We won't allow it. We're a close family at Blue Moon. Everyone likes you."

"Except Pam," she muttered.

"She's on thin ice with all of us." He took her hand and pressed his lips on her palm.

She held her breath as warmth spread across her skin like melting butter. Her heart hammered in her throat. For the first time in her life, a man's touch didn't feel like an assault. It felt safe. As if she were meant to be in this moment.

With him.

"Good night, Janelle." He released her hand. "Sleep well."

"You too." She slipped from the truck, missing the running board, and plummeted to the ground. "Ugh." She landed flat on her face.

"Oh shit." He raced around the front of the pickup and lifted her off the pavement. "Are you okay?"

She wiped her hair from her face. "Yeah. Just a bruised ego."

He laughed. "It's a long way down when you're what, five foot four?"

"I'm five five, thank you very much." She glanced up. "Although, I guess that's tiny next to the Jolly Green Giant."

"Oh my God. I'm not that tall."

"You've got to be over six feet."

"Six two." He smiled, holding her by the biceps. "Are you sure you're all right? Do you need help up to your apartment?"

"No. I'm fine."

He took her chin with his thumb and forefinger. His gaze tore deep into her soul.

"You're a beautiful woman, Janelle. Inside and out," he whispered. "I'm captivated by you." He leaned in and kissed her cheek, letting his lips linger.

God, she wanted more. Needed more.

Did she dare?

It wasn't ladylike to demand it.

In her culture, a woman never initiated contact. They never asked for anything. It wasn't their place.

It was for the man to dictate. And it was never about pleasure. At least not for a woman.

But this felt different. It felt good. It made her come alive. As if she'd been coasting through life, never really experiencing anything, only going through the motions of living.

She cupped his face and planted her mouth against his but had no idea what to do next.

She froze, horrified at what she'd just done.

Until his arms wrapped around hers and his tongue flicked inside her mouth, wrapping around hers in a forbidden dance. Melting against his body, she let instinct take over. This was what a kiss was supposed to be like. It was a hot fudge sundae on a warm summer day.

He pulled away, running his fingers through her hair, gazing into her eyes as if she were the only thing that mattered in the moment.

"I'll see you tomorrow." He smiled. "Go get some sleep. I'm sure you're tired." He leaned over, lifting her bag from the driveway.

Taking it, she turned and did her best to walk without falling over. She used the code to enter the garage versus using the outside stairs. Glancing over her shoulder, she waved before hitting the button. She darted up the stairs, tears filling her eyes.

How had this happened? She shouldn't allow

herself to become entangled with a man like Phoenix. Not only was he way out of her league, but she wasn't equipped to be dating anyone. She could barely comprehend the rules of the outside world, much less know how to navigate the uncharted waters of dating.

But she didn't think she could stop this if she tried.

And she didn't want to.

It was the fairy tale she so desperately had dreamed of ever since she'd said goodbye to Anne Marie and Jason.

5

"I can't be the one to fire Pam." Phoenix leaned back in the chair, still staring at the security footage. "And there's still the issue of bringing in the police. I have no idea how Janelle is going to react to that."

"Why didn't you tell Janelle what you suspected last night?" Maverick asked from the sofa across the room.

"Because I was concerned it was an ex-husband or boyfriend that had caught up to her based on some of her reactions to me and how she is in general." Phoenix raked his fingers through his hair. "I didn't want to spook her about someone slashing her tire until I knew that's what happened."

"I still can't believe Pam went to those lengths,"

Nelson said. "We all know she's got the hots for you, but that's taking things way too far."

"Hell, the second she showed up at Phoenix's place unannounced was going too far." Maverick stood and strolled toward the window. "We can't let this continue and what Pam did was criminal."

"It's vandalism, which is a misdemeanor. She'll get a ticket. A fine. She'll have to go to court, and Janelle can get a restraining order," Phoenix said. "Possibly, if she chooses to pursue it."

"Little brother, you have grounds for one as well." Nelson cocked a brow. "I highly recommend you file one."

"I'm considering it, but my first concern is Janelle." Phoenix peered over the screen. Pam leaned against the bar, chatting with one of the busboys. She hadn't been happy about the change in her schedule. Especially when she hadn't picked up the majority of Veronica's hours. She believed she was entitled to those. She begged and pleaded with Jack to tell her who had *stolen* them from her and all but accused Janelle. Pam went as far as to demand to see the new schedule, but Jack had told her that she would have to take that up with Phoenix and his brothers.

So far, all three of them had dodged the question through the breakfast rush while they sorted out the footage.

"Is Janelle coming to the restaurant?" Nelson asked.

"She doesn't feel comfortable driving my truck, so I asked Dad to pick her up," Phoenix said. "The only thing she knows right now is that there is a problem and we need her here."

"Have you called Jared?" Maverick rested his ass against the desk.

"No. I contacted Stacey. I thought a female state trooper might be less threatening to both women. She's in the parking lot. I asked her not to come up until after I had a chance to speak with Janelle."

"What if Janelle doesn't want to pursue anything?" Maverick asked.

"We're still firing Pam over this. We can't have employees bullying co-workers." Phoenix let out a long breath. "Not only is that behavior childish, but it's unacceptable."

"Agreed," Nelson said.

"Dad texted. They just pulled in. I need to let Jack know so he can keep Pam in the kitchen while Janelle comes up here."

"That's a good plan," Nelson said.

"Let me speak with her alone. I don't want her to feel like she's being ambushed." Phoenix shifted his gaze between his brothers.

"Fair enough." Maverick slapped his shoulder before making a beeline for the door.

"Call us if you need anything." Nelson followed his brother out the door and down into the bar area.

Phoenix watched from the window as they greeted their father and Janelle.

He studied her with a watchful eye. She appeared nervous as she fiddled with her bag strap. Slowly, she took the stairs, glancing twice over her shoulder.

"Hi," she said softly. "Your dad wouldn't tell me what was going on and I get the feeling this isn't about the new job responsibilities."

"Unfortunately, it's not." He stood, offering her his chair. "I have some disturbing information about your tire."

"What?"

"Sit. I want you to watch the security footage of the parking lot last night."

"Um, okay." She set her bag on the floor and scooted in close to the screen. "It's fuzzy and dark."

"It is. But it definitely shows exactly who slashed your tire."

"Huh?" She bolted out of the chair, sending it right into his leg.

"Humph."

"Sorry," she whispered.

"No worries." He waved his hand. "Just watch,

okay? And then we'll talk about what I'm going to do about it and what I think you should do."

She squared her shoulders and plopped into the chair.

"Ready?"

She nodded.

He pressed the return key and the footage rolled.

"Is that Pam?" Janelle asked. "Oh my God. What is she... did she take a knife to my tire?"

"She did." Phoenix tapped the escape key. "I should have told you last night that I suspected foul play, but I didn't want to scare you. It wasn't until I got confirmation about two hours ago that it was a clean cut that I pulled out the security footage and I saw that."

"Is Pam here?"

"She is, but she doesn't know you're here. I made sure that I had enough warning from my dad to keep you and Pam separate." He pulled up one of the other chairs and took Janelle by both hands. "Pam is going to be fired today. I can't have someone like that working here. We'd like you to file a police report against her and it would be in your best interest to obtain a restraining order."

"I don't want to cause problems."

"Jesus, Janelle. You're not. Pam is. You're

protecting yourself from the likes of that woman. Trust me when I say I'll also be filing against her."

"It's just going to make her angry and lash out more."

That was a reasonable point. "Only that tells her she can get away with stuff like that and she'll do it to someone else. Not on my watch. I can't force you to do anything, but I'm not letting this go. She's done some things to me that are upsetting and frankly, scare me a little, and that's tough to do."

"Can I watch it again?"

"Of course." He tapped the keyboard. "A friend of mine—and a neighbor—happens to be a state trooper. She's outside waiting for a text. When we're ready, she'll come in, view the footage, take our statements, and then interview Pam—"

"While I'm here?" Janelle asked with a quiver in her voice.

"You'll be safe. There will be no interaction between you and Pam. My brothers, me, and my dad will all make sure of that. Once Stacey has done her job, we will escort Pam off the premises and make sure she's gone before you leave this office. I will personally drive you home and take the rest of the day off to make sure she stays clear."

Janelle folded her hands in her lap and stared at them. "So, I will spend my time here in fear."

It was as if she'd resigned herself to that fact.

Which Phoenix didn't believe was true. Pam was a lot of things and while what she'd done bordered on crazy, Phoenix didn't think it could escalate. It wasn't the first time Pam had been mean to a new employee, although the worst thing she'd ever done had been giving the new girl the wrong schedule, making her look bad, as though she'd not come into work. It had been dealt with and Pam had been on her best behavior, until Janelle showed up.

Phoenix knew he needed to send his own message. That he wasn't going to let Pam bully him—or anyone—at his restaurant. He honestly believed this would be the end of it. Pam wasn't a physical threat, but she couldn't get away with tormenting anyone.

"Look. I understand that what happened is scary. However, Pam has never done anything like this before. She doesn't have a past history of violent behavior. She doesn't have a criminal record. No one has ever accused her of doing anything except being a mean girl." He held up his hand. "I'm not excusing her behavior. That's why I'm taking action." Pulling his cell from his pocket, he tapped the screen. "My friend Stacey is waiting for my text."

"The state trooper who lives down the street?"

He nodded. "Once Pam realizes she was caught

red-handed and faces the consequences of her actions, I know her well enough to know she'll back down."

"And what if she doesn't?"

Oh boy. That question alone told Phoenix that all his suspicions about Janelle having been in an abusive relationship were true. "That's why I want a restraining order. If she breaks it, she can be arrested. That should be enough to scare her into leaving both of us alone." He lifted her chin with his thumb. "It's going to be okay."

"I'm sorry. I feel a little foolish. I don't know how all this works and I don't like confrontation."

"No one does and trust me, I don't take any pleasure in doing this. But we have to." He quickly sent a message to Stacey, telling her to head straight to his office.

"I don't want to see Pam. Is that possible?"

"Yes," Phoenix said, squeezing her shoulder and staring out the window.

Stacey strolled through the door, decked out in her uniform. She stopped at the bar for a moment before making her way up the stairs.

Phoenix greeted her at the door. "Thanks for coming," he said. "You remember Janelle."

"I do." Stacey smiled. "I'm sorry we have to meet again under these circumstances."

Tentatively, Janelle rose, stretching out a shaky arm.

"I just came from the tire place and examined the damage. It was definitely done on purpose. That I can tell just from looking at the tire," Stacey said, pointing at the computer. "Mind if I take a look at the footage?"

"Please." Phoenix nodded.

Stacey positioned herself at the desk, using the mouse to click on the play button. She watched the video five times before standing tall and looping her fingers in her belt. "I'm going to need that footage as evidence."

"I've already made copies." Phoenix curled his fingers through Janelle's hand, grateful she didn't pull away. "You can have the original."

"I appreciate that." Stacey peered through the window. "You mentioned that Pam is still here and that you haven't said anything to her about this."

"That's correct. I thought it was best to let you handle this. We don't want to cause a scene or make things difficult for Janelle."

"Do you want to press charges?" Stacey stared at Janelle.

"I want to make sure she doesn't do anything like this again," Janelle said softly. "Phoenix mentioned something about a restraining order."

"Has she threatened you? Made any comments that have made you uncomfortable? Given you reason to fear that she'll harm you?" Stacey asked.

"She's not nice to me," Janelle said. "And slashing my tire does concern me."

"Understandable." Stacey widened her stance. "The value of the tire, unfortunately, makes this a misdemeanor. It's still an arrestable offense. I can charge her. She'll be taken down to the station, fingerprinted, the whole nine yards. But we won't keep her. She'll go to court where she'll be fined and since it's her first offense, she'll most likely be put on probation and do a little community service."

"I have more." Phoenix pulled up the text messages. "I believe this borders on harassment." He handed Stacey his cell.

She glanced at the screen, scrolling through the texts with wide eyes. "How long has this been going on?"

"A couple of weeks," Phoenix admitted. "It got worse after I hired Janelle."

"Not that's it's any of my business, but it will add a little color to the case. Is there something between you and Janelle?"

"Other than chemistry, not at this time." Phoenix squeezed Janelle's hand when she tried to tug it away. "Pam has been extremely jealous of Janelle since she walked through the door. I've made it perfectly clear what my boundaries are and Pam has broken them. Personally, I'd like a restraining order based on those texts and the fact that she slashed one of my employee's tires."

"I can file that for you, no problem. And one for Janelle too. Actually, I recommend it," Stacey said. "I've known Pam a long time. She's always been a jealous woman with attachment issues but has never carried it this far before."

"Wait, what?" Phoenix blinked. "She's done shit like this before?" That would change everything.

"No. Not really."

"Come on, Stacey. I need to know exactly what I'm dealing with," Phoenix said.

"About four years ago, her ex-boyfriend had to file a restraining order because she would constantly show up at his home. We were called a handful of times. It was benign. Nothing violent, but she did key his car."

"Shit," Phoenix mumbled. "That didn't come up in my search."

"Jesus, Phoenix. You've got to stop using your contacts to poke around in shit. Just because you're ex-military doesn't mean..." Stacey shook her head. "Regardless, you wouldn't find something like that because it's not active anymore. She backed off when shit got real. Arresting her will be enough."

"We hope." Phoenix turned his attention to Janelle. "You need to tell Stacey that you want to go ahead with the arrest."

"You mean I could let this go if I wanted to?" Janelle yanked her hand away. She inched closer to the window, peering down into the bar area. "I just want it all to go away."

"Honestly, I don't recommend doing that." Stacey turned, standing next to Janelle. She placed her hand on Janelle's biceps. "We're not dealing with a teenager who made a dumb mistake. She's a grown woman acting like a toddler. Let me do my job. It's not going to ruin her life, but it will teach her a lesson."

"All right," Janelle whispered.

"Where's Pam?" Stacey glanced over her shoulder.

"In the kitchen."

"I'll ask her to come outside so we don't make a scene in Blue Moon." Stacey didn't say another word. She left the office and made her way downstairs.

Phoenix took Janelle by the forearms. "I'm going to send my dad up here to stay with you."

"You're going to leave me?"

"No. But I'm the owner of this bar. I need to be downstairs and outside when this happens." He kissed her temple. "My father will take good care of you." He raced out the door and took the steps two at a time. Putting an end to this might give him a fighting chance at starting something with Janelle.

Something he wanted more than he realized.

"How ya holding up, kid?"

Janelle didn't turn her head away from the scene down below. "Scared," she managed.

"Don't be," Louis Snow said. "Stacey's one of the best cops out there. And she lives on our street. No matter what, you're safe."

For three years, Janelle had been looking over her shoulder, wondering if her father or Brother Jim had been searching for her. People didn't leave the church. She had watched a few try, but they always came back. Or they were found and brought back.

And punished for their betrayal.

Jason and Anne Marie had told her the real world could be cruel. But if she kept her head down and stayed out of trouble, she'd find good people along the way.

That's what she'd done, but she avoided close ties.

Until now.

Not that she'd call what she had with the Snow family close, but it was an entanglement that she'd never experienced before. The intense emotions were those that she craved her entire life. She'd always wanted to know what it would be like to be cared about. To have someone who put her needs before their own. Who didn't manipulate or twist reality for their own benefit.

That was Phoenix.

He was always helping others. She'd seen it firsthand. Paying part of someone's tab when they were short. Stopping to walk an elderly woman across the street. Running out to the store for his brothers and their families in the middle of the night. He was kind and caring like a prince in a fairy tale.

"Stop fretting over this," Louis said, wrapping a protective arm around her shoulders.

"I wish I knew what I did to her to make her slash my tire."

"Oh, sweetheart. You did nothing wrong. She's jealous."

"Everyone keeps saying that. But I don't understand why." Janelle had been told by Brother Jim that she was jealous of her other sister wives. That was the reason given for her so-called bad behavior. It was the only possible explanation as to why God constantly punished her. If she had been a better sister wife, she wouldn't have lost her babies. If she could have been kinder and gotten along like the other wives, she would have been blessed too. But that wasn't true. She didn't want to be like them or have the attention that they had. She wanted to fly under the radar. To blend into the walls of her own home.

The guilt for being grateful she didn't have a child consumed her in this moment. She wouldn't have been able to leave her own flesh and blood behind to suffer in that world. But could she have taken a kid with her and would she have been able to take care of them had she successfully left?

The answer was a resounding no.

"Because you have all the qualities she doesn't and more importantly, you've captured the attention of someone who isn't interested in her in a romantic way."

Janelle's heart lurched to her throat. Butterflies fluttered in her gut. She enjoyed every second of being with Phoenix. She had no idea what it meant to be a woman, and she still didn't, but in his presence, she had a desire to find out.

"I'm not sure what to say about that."

Louis chuckled. "If you want me to be totally honest with you, I don't know either. Phoenix has never been this smitten before. Sure, he's brought girls around that he's liked, but his eyes have never twinkled like the stars lining a summer sky. When he looks at you, it reminds me of when I first met his mother."

She opened her mouth to respond, but Pam appeared from the kitchen, looking shocked to see a police officer.

"We don't have to watch this," Louis said.

"I want to."

"I'm not sure that's a good idea." He tugged at her shoulder. "If she looks up, she can see you."

Reaching deep within herself, she found the same courage she had when she left the compound. "I might be naive when it comes to how all this works, but I'm the one pressing charges. I'm sure she's going to know it was me anyway."

"That's true," Louis said.

Pam shook her head. She raised her arms up, then lowered them to her sides.

Stacey pointed to the door.

Pam folded her arms across her chest.

Phoenix and his brothers stood near the bar, a few feet from the scene.

"I kind of wish I could hear what was happening," she said.

"It's looking a little like she's arguing with Stacey, which isn't advisable. She's one badass... oh shit."

Stacey unhooked her handcuffs.

"My boys are going to be pissed if Stacey has to arrest her in the bar."

Janelle leaned closer. She couldn't believe how fascinated she'd become with what had unfolded down below. She envisioned what it might be like to watch her father and Brother Jim arrested.

When she lived in the compound, deep down she understood what they were doing was wrong, but she couldn't put it to words. Living in the outside world gave her that knowledge. However, she still couldn't bring herself to tell her story to anyone.

Much less the police.

She swallowed.

Recently, she'd seen something in the news about her father's church and how an investigation about child brides had been opened. But since then, she hadn't seen anything and she was too afraid to go searching for it. She didn't really understand the internet or how it worked. All she knew was that was how people could find her if she wasn't careful.

"Looks like Pam is going to put up a little bit of a fight," Louis said.

Stacey took Pam by the arms and pushed her against the bar. It was rough, and Janelle thought it might have been unnecessary, but she had no idea what had been said.

Everyone around them had taken a few steps back, including Phoenix and his brothers.

Jack had cleared out what few customers had remained.

"Resisting an officer is never a good idea," Louis said. "It won't help her case when she goes in front of a judge."

"I just want this to be over with." Janelle jerked, taking a step back when Pam glanced toward the window, locking gazes.

Pam's stare horrified Janelle. It was as if she were looking into one of her sister wives' eyes after she'd been scolded by Brother Jim and about to be taken to task by them for something as little as not putting a dish in the proper place.

Nelson and Maverick followed Stacey and Pam out the door, while Phoenix turned and jogged up the stairs.

Janelle wiggled her fingers. A small part of her wished she could speak up about her past. About what she'd endured. What she'd run from and why. And she wanted to find the courage to finally go to the authorities and put an end to her father.

But at what cost?

And would it do any good?

"Well, that was exciting," Louis said.

"A little too much." Phoenix leaned against the

doorjamb. "I can't believe Pam tried to resist. She actually told Stacey to fuck off."

"You've got to be kidding me." Louis kept his arm around Janelle like a father would. "Why would she do that?"

"When Stacey asked her to go outside so as not to embarrass her, Pam lost it. She denied slashing the tire. Called me a liar and accused me of doctoring whatever proof I had." Phoenix raked his fingers through his hair. "Stacey said she'll still be out in an hour or two. She'll let me know when Pam's left the station so we can go file our restraining orders, but she's going to tell Pam that it's done. She can't come near Blue Moon, our home, or either of us, or she'll be arrested again."

"Hopefully this is the end of it," Louis said.

"People don't change their stripes that easily." Janelle had heard Jason use that quote a dozen times in reference to her father whenever she would try to defend him and his actions.

She'd tell Jason about all the good things her dad had done for the community. How he hadn't always been about marrying off young girls to older men.

Jason would come back with proof that her father had always been that way.

Her retort would come in the form of how good

plural marriage could be and that sometimes a few years age difference didn't matter.

Jason didn't disagree, except that no fifteen-year-old should be forced to marry anyone.

Janelle couldn't argue that point.

And the church had been marrying young girls for a long time.

"She's showing her true colors, which have always been there," she said. Another Jason quote.

"You say that as though you're speaking from experience." Phoenix arched a brow.

Jason once told her that she could always speak her truth through someone else's eyes if she wanted. "I had a friend who lived through an abusive relationship. He didn't start out being mean or hitting her, but that's where it ended. And there were signs, but she had to look back from a distance to see them." It was strange to have this newfound sense of empowerment. Anne Marie told her it would come. That she'd find it at an odd time in her life. Well, she needed it now because she didn't want to leave Lake George.

She'd driven out of the storm and into a little piece of heaven.

Pam wasn't going to force her to leave it.

"I'm sorry your friend had to go through that," Phoenix said. "It's no way to live. I hope she's in a good place now."

"She is." Janelle held his gaze. He was a smart man. She could only hope he didn't see right through the lie.

"Good." Phoenix reached for her hand. "Let's get out of here."

"And go where?" she asked.

"Besides the police station? I don't know. But I'm taking the rest of the day off. Maybe a boat ride. Anything to get our minds off what just went down." Phoenix smiled.

"Sounds like a plan," Louis said. "Call me if you need me." He waved his hand over his head as he strolled down the steps.

"Are you okay?" Phoenix wrapped his arms around her, heaving her to his chest.

"Yeah," she managed, resting her arms on his strong shoulders. She gazed into his deep blue eyes, losing herself in the moment. She'd watched so many romantic movies. She'd fantasized about having a man sweep her off her feet, knowing that none of that was real.

Only, Phoenix was flesh and blood. He was standing right in front of her and his lips were so close she could feel the heat pouring from his skin.

"Are you going to kiss me again?" she whispered.

"For the record, you kissed me."

Before she could respond, his mouth covered hers

in a hot, wet dance that ignited a flame deep in her soul. He lifted her feet right off the floor, holding her tight as his tongue gripped hers, dancing and swirling around like a tornado tearing across the plains.

Someone cleared their throat in the background.

Gently, he set her back down.

"Sorry to interrupt," Nelson said. "But some of us have work to do and I need the office."

He ran his thumb over her lower lip. "It's all yours. We're going for a boat ride."

"Enjoy." Nelson laughed. "Don't do anything I wouldn't do."

"Shut up," Phoenix mumbled, taking her by the hand and guiding her down the steps. "Don't listen to my stupid brothers."

"I have one question about you and your brothers."

"Yeah. What's that?"

"Your dad mentioned on the way over that when you were kids, you'd have a lemonade and cookie stand."

"Oh, good grief. He did not tell that story."

"So, it's true. You wore a dress, believing it would sell more cookies."

He smacked his forehead. "I was five years old. Maverick was seven and Nelson was nine. Those two clowns told me one of us had to because people wouldn't buy cookies from anyone other than a girl. They had me believing that for an entire year. Assholes."

"You dad said there are pictures." A warmth spread across her belly. This was what it was like to have real friends. To belong.

He paused midstep at the main door. "I will hurt my brothers if they ever share that picture."

"Aw, come on. I bet it's cute."

"It's embarrassing."

"A small boy wearing a dress is nothing short of adorable." She stepped around him and opened the door. "It can't be any worse than when I fell off the back of my daddy's truck into a pile of horse shit." She left out the fact that her father had pushed her because she wasn't a godly child, but what difference did that make? The point was to share a story that could be remotely funny.

And a kid covered in shit should be funny.

"That's gross and hilarious at the same time."

"I smelled for weeks." She plugged her nose.

"I bet." He opened the door to his shiny sports car.

"Can I ask you a personal question?"

"Of course," he said.

"How old are you?" She knew he was a little older, making her uncomfortable. She was an adult. Free to make her own choices. But her upbringing tainted so much of her world view, his possible age did give her pause.

"Thirty-eight."

That made him twelve years older. That was a lot of living. She bit down on her lower lip.

"Does that bother you?"

"It's not so much your age as it's the fact you've lived this colorful life with various experiences. I've been sheltered."

"I saw your resume. Moving from one town to the next for the last few years isn't sheltered."

"My childhood was," she admitted. Opening up wasn't something she was used to doing. However, if she was committed to staying in Lake George, living above Phoenix's garage, working at Blue Moon, and letting him kiss her some more, she needed to open up, even if it was only half-truths and made-up stories she'd learned. "My parents were strict. They didn't let me do a lot; I was a shy kid. It wasn't until after they died that I broke from my shell and started venturing out of the community I grew up in."

"I hate to break it to you, but I had figured that out already." He tucked a piece of hair behind her ear. "I've seen and done a lot because of my military career and some days I feel older than dirt. I look at you and see this young woman who has yet to experience so much and it makes me think I shouldn't be having the thoughts and feelings I am. But then I realize there's one thing I have absolutely no experience in."

"What's that?"

"Having a real relationship with a woman and you're the first person I've met whom I can see myself doing that with."

Her heart dropped to her toes. Her lips parted and a gasp escaped. She quickly regained her composure. "This is all new to me. I've had one relationship; honestly, it wasn't a very good one."

"I can't say I've ever had a good or bad one. I just haven't stayed with a girl long enough to call it that." He kissed her cheek. "But I'd like to find out what we could be." He gave her a little nudge into the passenger seat.

Her mouth defied her and curled into a smile. What could have been one of the worst days of her new start had turned into another new beginning.

6

Janelle held her glass of wine. She leaned against the railing on the sundeck. The moon and the stars lit up the night sky. She loved coming out onto the dock after the sun had set. Hell, sitting on the upper deck any time of day, outside of work, was her favorite pastime. It was strange to enjoy a little downtime. While she still worried Pam would jump out from behind a tree, after six or seven days of not seeing her anywhere, she was starting to believe Phoenix and his philosophy. That Pam had been scared enough about the consequences of her actions. That messing with Janelle wasn't worth it and it certainly wouldn't change Phoenix's mind.

She raised her fingers to her lips. Over the course

of the last week, he'd kissed her two or three times a day. Usually, a stolen one in the morning when she came into work, since he always got there before she did. A second one when she left. If she was lucky, she'd get a third one at home. That one usually lasted a lot longer. But that's as far as things went.

She had to admit, she missed working the night shift. Jack was fun to work with and the night crowd was so lively. But Janelle really enjoyed the position and she had at least two night shifts over the weekends. She'd also brought up that two of the college girls returning preferred earlier hours. She managed to talk the brothers into reworking how her position looked as interim manager.

Only time would tell if it was a good idea or not.

The crickets sang a symphony while the waves from a boat gently lapped at the shoreline. She sucked in a deep breath.

Phoenix wasn't supposed to close this evening. She glanced at her watch. It was half past ten and he wasn't home. She raised her glass. Two sips left. That's how long she had until she'd head up to her apartment and give up on Phoenix.

She took the first sip, slowly letting it roll down her throat. Wine had become something she savored. She was careful of how much she drank. She knew when she was getting close to having too much. She understood the effects and didn't want to push the envelope. But the flavors were to die for. The adultness of merely holding the glass made her almost forget how submissive she'd been her entire life.

Flashes of her sister wives, her siblings, her mothers, and all the other women living in that compound pounded her brain like a hammer beating a nail until it was so wedged into the wood it couldn't be pulled out if anyone tried.

Janelle was free. So free that when she'd become a victim to a crime, she'd been so empowered to report it. She downed her last sip. She might not have if it hadn't been for Phoenix and everyone else at Blue Moon. Janelle had what Jason told her to go looking for.

A support system.

People who would look out for her in the right way. A positive way.

None of those women or children had choices. They were prisoners, even the ones who promoted the church. Believed in its teachings.

Because they were brainwashed.

That was no way to live.

In that moment, it felt like the weight of the world was on her shoulders. She couldn't bear the responsibility. It couldn't be on her to come forward.

One woman had left when Janelle had been maybe fourteen. This woman, Audrey, escaped with her seventeen-year-old daughter, Tara, who was ordered to marry an older man.

They told their story.

Nothing happened.

Except Tara came back.

It was the strangest thing. Tara showed up one day without her mother. There were no televisions in the compounds, so no one knew what the mom was telling the outside world. But Janelle's dad—and Tara—told everyone that the mom had kidnapped her and the girl found her way home.

That girl looked freshly battered and beaten.

For weeks.

She married that older man, and Janelle watched Tara become a shell. She only spoke if spoken too. She walked through the compound with her head down and her hands clasped. She became the epitome of respect. The example for how all women should behave.

Seen, not heard.

Tara looked as though she was the most miserable young girl on the planet.

Janelle got to spend a little time with her and finally got her to speak about her mother and what happened.

It wasn't the same tale that the elders had told. No. The elders' security had found her and her mother—something that Janelle didn't even know existed—and Tara was snatched up right away.

Fear crawled across her spine. She quickly glanced over her shoulder, half expecting to see her father's army. All she saw was the darkness surrounding Phoenix's empty house. She turned, keeping her focus on the light of the moon dancing across the waters. It was peaceful. Warm. Comforting.

Even in the wake of the horror and death that Tara had told.

That made her father—and his church—murderers.

At first, Janelle didn't believe Tara. While Janelle had been struggling with her dad and his teachings, she had yet to be married off and she hadn't suffered. She didn't like the changes that were being put into place. Everyone wearing the same clothes. The girls having to wear their hair the same way and not being allowed to cut it. They had never had televisions, but they had some access to the outside world.

That was all cut off now.

No influences.

No trips with the adults to the grocery store or anywhere.

Janelle wondered if Tara missed her mother and

made up the story. Or, as her father had decided, Tara was being tempted by the devil. Janelle gripped the railing and sucked in a deep breath. Tara had been beaten into submission. When Janelle left, that woman had birthed three children and almost never spoke, except to her kids and her husband. She did exactly what she was told. She'd once again become a model sister wife.

Only, that's not what plural marriage was all about. At least not what Janelle remembers had been taught and what she'd seen when she was four and five years old.

Or what she'd seen along the way when she stayed in one community where five families practiced plural marriage. That had been an interesting place to stay.

She set her glass on the small table and wiggled her fingers. She needed to purge this insane thinking. The thoughts stemmed from guilt because she'd been unable to stand up for herself and in the process potentially prevent it from happening to someone else in the future.

But she'd been a coward when she ran.

And she still was.

Jason and Anne Marie were paying it forward by getting people out. They didn't force anyone. They offered assistance to those who wanted it when they were ready. Once Janelle got out, she realized that her dad knew exactly who Jason and Anne Marie were. That he was prepared for them and others like them. It was a weird feeling to know that her dad was willing to go to war with the outside world, not with words like he professed, but with guns.

And worse.

Killing his own to prove a point.

A hand came down on her shoulder. "Hey."

She jumped, spinning around, shoving whoever had touched her.

"Whoa. It's just me, Phoenix." He stood there with both hands up in the air, showing his palms. "I'm sorry. I didn't mean to spook you. I honestly thought you heard those creaky steps."

"I didn't hear anything." She brushed her hair from her face. "I hope I didn't hurt you."

He laughed. "I'm fine. Luckily, I hadn't poured my wine yet." He turned and pointed to the bottle on the far table. "You must have been deep in thought. I set that down along with a cheese board."

Tell one person your story. It will help you heal. Those were Anne Marie's words. She mentioned that it didn't have to be in the vein of sharing it with the world. Or bringing her father's church down. It was just about unburdening herself of the pain she carried deep in her soul. To get them out of her heart so she could live her life to the fullest. Have all her dreams and leave that life in her rearview once and for all.

Could Phoenix be the one person she could trust with the horrors of her past? Would it be too much to ask of him to share that part of her life with?

"Wow, you're still thinking about something deep." He took her empty glass and guided her toward the lounge chairs.

The sundeck had become one of her favorite places to spend her free time. It was peaceful, even when boats zoomed up and down the shore.

He lifted the bottle of wine and poured before settling into one of the lounge chairs.

She followed suit, holding the glass close to her chest. If she drank too much more, she might find out what it was like to be drunk. She wasn't sure that was a good idea. "It's easy to get lost in thought out here."

"That's so true." He lifted a cracker and placed a piece of meat and a slice of cheese on top. He plopped it in his mouth and devoured it. "I've spent a lot of time contemplating my life up here," he said. "What put that scowl on your pretty face?"

She rubbed her forehead.

"Are you still worried about Pam? Because I think we put that to bed. I heard through one of her friends that Pam went out on a date with some guy.

She's moved on. She won't be bothering either one of us anymore."

"It's not that." A thick lump formed in Janelle's throat. "I mean, I do worry about running into her in places." Janelle never went anywhere besides Blue Moon, the grocery store, and home. But Pam wasn't someone she wanted to have any conversation with. While she'd done what she needed to in order to protect herself, she didn't know if she had the strength to defend herself one-on-one. Even with words. "I was thinking about my parents and my home back in New Mexico."

"Is that where you're originally from?"

She nodded. Her heart beat so fast it hurt.

"You mentioned your parents had passed? How old were you?"

She closed her eyes. "I wasn't truthful about that," she whispered. "My mother did die when I was young, but my father is still alive."

"Why did you need to lie to me about that?"

She blinked and glanced to the sky, which was filled with bright stars. She hoped they would give her the courage to get through this without either telling more lies or falling apart. "I've only told two other people about what happened to me." She let out a nervous laugh. "And truth be told, I didn't tell them. They knew what was happening because they both had lived it, just differently."

Phoenix swung his legs to the side, leaned over, and took her glass from her hands. "I'm going to try to make this as easy as possible for you." He kissed her palm. "I told you that tomorrow I wanted to take you somewhere as a surprise."

"That makes me a little nervous. I don't like surprises."

"Well, it's a strange one because Foster, Brandi's brother-in-law, and I both volunteer a lot at a women's shelter. That's where we're going tomorrow."

She cocked her head. "Why?"

"Because I thought it might be good for you." He lowered his chin. "I don't want to tell your story for you, but I know the signs. I've seen battered women and I can tell when someone has been in that situation."

She jerked her hand away, gasping, covering her mouth.

"I'm not judging. This is a safe space. I'm certainly not pressuring you to tell me anything. That's up to you. But tomorrow was about me showing you that I understand."

"My past is that obvious to you? To everyone?"

"Not everyone and I don't know what happened, only that someone hurt you."

"How can you tell?" Her lungs burned with every breath. The desire to run muscled into her mind. Packing up her things had become easy. Moving from town to town and finding a job and a place to live hadn't been hard. She'd learned to live on very little.

She could do it all again if she had to.

But she didn't want to. Lake George had been the first place she landed where she felt like she could make it her home. Phoenix and his brothers had made her feel welcome. Brandi and Hensley treated her like a part of the family. They checked in with her regularly. Asked if she needed anything and genuinely seemed as though they liked her and Janelle enjoyed their company.

And their kids.

It differed from spending time with her sister wives' children or families in the compound.

"It comes from all my time working with women like you," he said softly. "I feel like I might have stalled the conversation by trying to make you feel more comfortable. I'm sorry."

"The problem is I doubt you've ever come across anyone like me before."

"I've seen a lot at the shelter."

She'd never heard the word *cult* before until she'd left the compound. She was born and raised in the religion. Kept from the outside world and sheltered from their opinion of what her father had done to the church. She knew the people on the other side of the walls wanted to destroy them and the work of God. But she didn't understand why, except they were the devil.

"You might want to buckle up for this story." It was now or never. She snagged the glass and took three big gulps. She'd heard it called liquid courage at the bar before, and right now, she needed it. Every fiber of her being screamed to release the beast. To purge the burden that she'd carried for the last three years. "My life isn't something that most people have ever experienced."

"My career isn't anything that the average person could comprehend. I doubt you'll shock me."

She blew out a puff of air. "My great-grandfather was a preacher of a fundamentalist Christian church. When I was young, while the doctrine was strict, it allowed for plural marriage."

"Excuse me? As in a man having more than one wife?"

"Exactly."

"That's not right."

"Growing up, I didn't know any better. And to be honest, while it isn't something I would want to ever experience again—"

"Again? You were married to a man who had more than one wife?"

"Can you let me get through this? I've never told it to anyone and you're making it harder for me."

"I'm sorry. Go ahead."

"Polygamy by itself isn't necessarily bad. I've seen it work when everyone is a willing participant. But it comes with its own set of challenges. However, things in the church began to change when my father took over. It got stricter. We already had little contact with the outside world, and it became less. When my biological mother died, my father started arranging marriages. He said that God spoke directly to him and in order for our flock to grow and spread the word, this was what the good Lord wanted us to do."

"Jesus. He married you off when you were underage, didn't he?"

She nodded.

"Motherfucker." Phoenix ran his fingers through his hair and abruptly stood. He turned and gripped the railing. "How old were you?"

"Seventeen," she whispered.

"And when you finally left?"

"Twenty-three," she managed.

"Was both your father and husband abusive?"

"Yes."

"Did you ever report them?" He glanced over his shoulder.

She shook her head. "I know I should have. This whole thing with Pam has me thinking about all the girls still stuck in that world. Some don't know what's happening to them is wrong."

"If they were born and raised in a cult, how could they?" He closed the gap, snagging his wine. He lifted it to his lips and downed it one gulp before pouring more and polishing that off. "I can understand your need to get out and put it behind you. I don't fault you for that. I've worked with dozens of women who, for whatever reason, couldn't or wouldn't press charges. They wanted to disappear. Not to mention that sometimes the system doesn't work as well as it should and the perpetrator often ends up back on the streets."

"Like Pam?"

"She's not the best example because she's not violent. Or at least she's not showing signs of that. But yes. Her crime was a misdemeanor. But if she does it again, and it's reported, she'll be in more trouble." He cocked his head. "What your father and husband did is a felony. That's entirely different, especially if they are still doing it." He eased back into the chair. "How did you get out?"

This was the part of the story that would take

more work to tell. She sipped her wine and contemplated where to start. "I was never legally married."

"That doesn't make it okay."

"Trust me. I know that," she said. "I was wife number four. A year after I was married, my father brought a sixteen-year-old to my husband. It wasn't the first time I'd seen that. I wanted nothing to do with it, but I was pregnant and I felt trapped."

"You have a child?"

"No. I had lost that baby." She sniffled. "As a matter of fact, I had three miscarriages and one stillbirth." The words tumbled from her mouth like an ice cube. Cold and hard. She had no emotion left for what happened. Of course she cared about her unborn children. She'd been devastated by losing those babies. She believed she'd been ungodly. Unholy.

"Jesus, I'm so sorry."

"It's okay. I believe I've come to terms with it. In the long run, it turned out to be a blessing." She squared her shoulders. "But between what happened with Pam and seeing something on the news about my father's church—"

"Wait a second. Is your father Adam Weiss? The leader of the Fundamentalist Christ Revolution?"

"How do you know about him?"

"I watch the news every day. I saw that someone accused the FCR of crimes against minors."

"When I was a toddler, the church came under fire under my grandfather's rule. It all had to do with plural marriage back then and we were living in Utah where at the time it was criminalized. It's not in other states. But my grandfather didn't believe in child brides. He always thought eighteen was the right age. And he never arranged marriages. Those were choices between men, women, and God. My father is the one who changed all that."

Phoenix let out a long sigh. "You certainly know a lot about the law. Did you understand all that living in the FCR, or was that something you've learned in the last three years?"

"I didn't have an education outside of our bible when I left. I could read and write. I had a basic understanding of math. But I knew nothing of the real world. It's all accumulated knowledge."

"I'll be honest. I expected either a traumatic childhood or an abusive ex. But this is a lot to digest." He ran his hand over his face. "What made you decide to leave and are you worried at all about them finding you?"

"It was the way I was treated when I lost my last baby." It amazed her the strength that soared through her veins while she told her story. Anne Marie told her it would empower her and that's exactly what it did. "And I had met someone at the hospital who had once been in an offshoot of my father's church. She had escaped and she offered to help. I took her and her husband up on it and I didn't once look back. I never stayed longer than a few months in any one town because, yes. I'm scared that if my father or spiritual husband ever found me, they might try to kidnap me or force me back home. I've seen women who had left return. It's never good."

"I imagine it's not." He took both her hands. "You're a courageous woman for doing what you did."

"I would have been more courageous if I had told my story to the authorities or done what my friends do and helped other girls escape."

"Sometimes you have to take care of yourself before you can help anyone else. You weren't ready. And as I've learned over the years, you can't save everyone because some people don't want to be saved."

"I swear, one of my sister wives believed wholeheartedly in my father's message. When he came to her telling her that her daughter, who was only fifteen, was called to marry my dad of all people, she handed her over without question. She was proud and honored. I was horrified."

"I'm sorry. That's disgusting and I have no words."

"It was hard to live."

"I'm going to have my mom check in with her contacts at the FBI to see if they know anything."

"Poking around in the FCR isn't a good idea. They have found ways to hide behind religion and their right to practice it. Their followers will lie in order to protect their place in heaven because they believe they have to, even if their hearts are telling them something else."

He pressed his finger against her lips. "I'm going to ask you a really tough question and trust me when I say, it pains me to even speak the words." He cleared his throat. "Did your spiritual husband, or whatever he was, force you into his bed?"

"It was our duty as his wives."

"That's bullshit." His eyes narrowed and his face hardened. "Sex is not an obligation. It's not a husband's right to take his wife anytime he pleases. It's a privilege. And that works both ways. In any relationship. If you're not in the mood or don't want to, you have the right to say no and a real man would never force you. That's called rape and it's criminal. So is having sex with a minor."

"I know." She clasped her hands, rested them in her lap, and lowered her gaze.

"Don't do that," he said firmly but with a kind and

soft tone. "It's a form of submission and it breaks my heart."

She rubbed her hands up and down her legs. "I have no intention of living that way again. I've worked hard to become my own person. But I've also tried not to stand out in the crowd. I've never wanted to be noticed and that's happened since I've come here. It's a weird thing to love a place so much. To become attached so quickly. To have real friends for the first time in my life. And yet I still feel that pull to run."

"I can understand that." He leaned back. "I want you to know that you're safe with me. I would never do anything intentionally to hurt you."

"I believe that about you. And everyone in your family. It's why I didn't leave the moment Pam started causing trouble."

"I'm glad." He held her gaze. "This might not be the right time to say this. I'm attracted to you. I like you. A lot. And when I came home tonight, I had this idea where I'd sweep you off your feet. That we'd have this big romantic night and things would end with you spending the night in my bed."

She swallowed. Hard. His raw honesty about what he wanted—desired—not only startled her, but it sent a confusing warmth across her body. Part of her thought she should be angry at him for believing that could even be a possibility. However, if she were being honest, it was exactly what she wanted but couldn't ask for or even act on.

"I guess my confession ruined all that."

"No." He tapped his chest. "That hurts my heart that you had to suffer all that pain alone. But it's the realization that at twenty-six, that world when it comes to relationships and sex is probably all you've ever known."

"Oh," she managed.

He shifted, catching her gaze. "Am I wrong?"

She shook her head. Tears burned her eyes as they plummeted down her cheeks.

"Shit. I didn't mean to make you cry." He lifted her right off the chair and onto his lap. Wrapping his strong arms around her, he held her close.

That only made it worse. She couldn't stop the floodgates if she tried. She nestled her face into his neck.

"Okay, sweetheart. Let it all out. I've got you."

Fisting his shirt, she let the emotions bleed out. All the years of her father telling her no man was going to want her if she didn't become closer to God. Of her father taking a belt to her for asking simple questions about why they did the things they did.

Tears poured out for the babies she'd lost.

The sister wives and young children still being held, some against their will.

The whole godforsaken thing until her tank became empty.

He stood, holding her in his arms, carrying her toward the stairs.

"Where are you taking me?"

"Inside. You need to sleep." He pressed his lips against her temple. They were warm, soft, and sucked away all the pain that lingered.

"Okay." She closed her eyes, doing her best to forget everything, except Phoenix.

7

"Hey, Mom." Phoenix lifted his coffee mug and stared out into the darkness. A hint of light echoed through the sky, but it would be another hour before the sun peeked over the mountaintops. "Thanks for calling."

"I told you I'd call as soon as I learned anything."

He tugged at the slider. The cool air hit his skin. He leaned against the railing, taking a sip. "I appreciated the text before startling me awake." He didn't want to mention that he'd lain next to Janelle all night while she slept. He worried she might wake up and freak out whenever he dozed off.

First for being in his bed.

And second for him being right next to her.

"I have to ask. What's your interest in this group?"

"I know I don't have to say this, but it needs to stay within the family group," he said. "But Janelle was once a member. And not just any member. Her father is Adam Weiss."

"Of all the things going through my mind, that was not one of them," his mom said.

"It was bad for her, Mom. I mean, worse than anything I've ever seen or dealt with in all my years of volunteering, and I don't think she told me half of it."

"Well, I'm glad she felt comfortable telling you anything and even more happy that she got out."

"You and me both," he said. "So, what did you find out?"

"The FCR has been on the FBI's radar for a few years now, but they haven't had anyone come forward or had enough evidence to issue a search warrant. The church is well protected with their religious freedoms. For the most part, they don't bother anyone. They don't go around recruiting people."

"According to Janelle, they marry off teenagers to old men."

"That's one of the rumors, but no one has been able to prove it. This latest allegation is about a husband abusing one of his wives. She's of legal age, though she's only twenty-one."

"Does she have any children?"

"Two," his mom said. "One of the kids got sick

and she was able to leave with the help of some guy by the name of Jason Wilcox and his wife, Anne Marie. At first, she was willing to press charges, but my friend told me she went back to the compound and is now recanting her story."

"What about the other woman?"

"Her husband was arrested for assault and battery. She's going through with the charges but isn't speaking out against the church. She has no sister wives. Both she and her husband are twenty-two. No children. She wasn't raised in the church and neither was her husband. They joined when they were eighteen. She stated they both were addicted to drugs and FCR saved their lives. But her husband changed and when he wanted to take on a second wife, which she wasn't into, he flipped and beat the shit out of her."

"How old was the second wife?"

"That's where things get vague. The accuser doesn't say. She said it was a concept and not a given. My friend at the FBI doesn't believe it. Either way, there's insufficient information to get a search warrant. The domestic dispute will be dealt with. It will make waves because of the secrecy that swarms around FCR, but the Feds have nothing."

"Janelle could give them a ton of shit, but I wouldn't want to pressure her. When she started telling her story, she was strong. Confident even. And then she broke down and bawled for hours."

"Where is she now?"

"Asleep," he said, leaving it at that.

"In the main house?" His mother probed further, which he shouldn't have been surprised, but he didn't really want to get into it. However, he wasn't going to lie.

"Yes."

"Is there something going on between the two of you?"

"Not like that." He lifted his mug and took a long sip. "Although, things were heading in that direction before I kind of pushed her into telling me about her past."

"I can imagine that would make you pull back."

"Her having been abused isn't why," he said. "It's because she's never experienced what things should be like. She's never been with anyone else but her asshole perverted old man of a husband." He raked a hand over the top of his head. "And what honestly creeped me out is he's not much older than me."

"Honey, you're comparing apples to oranges. First, age is just a number and if you care about this woman, don't let those ten or twelve years get in the way of that."

"Hard not to considering what she's been through."

"Perhaps, but have you asked her how she feels about your age difference? Or you, for that matter?"

"Nope," he said. "All we've shared is some great conversation and a few kisses. It's not a great romance or anything."

"Phoenix. I know you. And I'm not blind," his mom said. "I've never seen you this attached to a woman before. Ever."

"This is confusing." He leaned against the railing. "I've spent my entire adult life void of emotional ties. It's not that I avoided them; it's that they never presented themselves. The first time I have real feelings for a lady, she's not only from a cult and was in an abusive past relationship, but that's all the experience she has?"

"Sounds like you're feeling responsible and utterly terrified at the same time."

"Something like that." Growing up, Phoenix had always been incredibly close to his dad, but it was his mother whom he went to for most of his big life decisions. He couldn't explain why. When his brothers were discussing losing their virginity with their dad, Phoenix was having that conversation with his mom. Most would find that awkward and uncomfortable.

Phoenix found it comforting and enlightening at the same time.

"She's a grown woman with a past you can't even begin to fathom, even if you empathize. Please don't project your feelings to her without having a conversation first. She might need to take things slow or maybe move fast. Put her in the driver's seat."

"I can do that," he said. "But I also want her to consider telling her story to the Feds."

"That's a big ask to become the poster child for bringing down an entire church, especially when it's her father who leads it."

A shadow moved across the kitchen. "I have to go. She's awake, but will you send me what you have?"

"Doing that now. If I find out anything else, I'll let you know."

"Thanks, Mom. I love you."

"Love you too, kiddo."

He tapped the screen and opened the slider. "Good morning."

She jumped.

"Shit. Sorry. I didn't mean to scare you."

"It's okay." She waved her hand. "I've been a little disoriented since I woke up. I had no idea I slept here all night."

"I didn't want to wake you, so I let you stay in my bed."

"Both sides were pulled down." She cocked her head. "Where did you stay?"

"I couldn't leave your side either." He held his hands up. "But I was a gentleman. I swear. I just wanted to be there in case you needed me."

She climbed up on the stool. "It's funny. When I was supposedly married, Jim never stayed in my room. I don't know if he slept all night with any of my other sister wives. I guess he did. But he came in and—"

"Yeah. I don't need the details."

"I wasn't going to give them to you." She arched a brow. "My point was, for as long as I was married, I never spent an entire night with my husband. So last night would have been a first and I want to thank you for making it a kind, safe, and nice memory, even if I don't recollect any of it."

He laughed, enjoying how she found a silver lining. "Would you like some coffee?"

"I would love some, thank you," she said. "I'm sorry last night ended the way it did. I'm glad I told you. I know it's a lot for anyone to hear, but it was something I've needed to share with someone."

"I'm grateful you trust me." He placed a mug under the coffee maker and pressed the button. "I'd like to ask you another incredibly personal question and I'm hoping for an honest answer."

She tucked her hair behind her ears. "I don't really want to go through it all again."

"There's no reason for us to rehash any of that," he said. "It has to do with my feelings for you."

"Oh." She blinked, fiddling with her hair.

He pushed the mug across the counter. She lifted it, blew into the steaming brew, and took a short sip. She didn't care that it burned her lip. She might not be worldly enough to know that his kisses meant something other than friendship.

"I won't insult you and say that what you told me last night didn't affect me deep to my core." He sat on the stool next to her, holding her gaze intently. "But it doesn't change how I feel. But there's something you need to know about me and my past."

"What's that?"

"I've never been in a long-term loving relationship. Hell, I've never been in love before. I've gone from one fling to the next. I haven't cared enough about any one woman to make a go of it. You're really throwing me for a loop because you're making me rethink my life in terms I never have before. I want to know if there's something between us, but I'm concerned about a few things."

"You mean my past has you freaked out."

He took her hands and kissed them. "That's not what I'm saying."

"Then what?"

Reaching out, he ran his thumb across her lower lip. "May I kiss you?"

"Yes," she whispered.

He took her mouth in a tender kiss. He had intended it to only last a minute. Maybe two. But he found himself wrapping his arms around her, pulling her to his chest, and deepening the kiss to the point it was wild and out of control.

Her fingernails dug into his shoulder blades. She leaned into his chest with her knee between his legs.

It took all his resolve not to lift her into his arms and carry her back to bed.

Cupping her face, he reluctantly broke off the kiss. "I want to be with you, but I'm afraid."

"Why?"

He pressed his forehead to hers and sighed. "I don't know what I'm doing. I care about you and I don't want you to get hurt. I'm terrified to say the wrong thing in this moment."

"I've been pregnant four times. I know what sex is."

"You're killing me," he whispered. "What you had with your husband wasn't making love, much less sex. It was rape and you're never going to get me to believe it was anything else."

"Okay, but I do have an idea of what it's supposed

to be like. It's not like I haven't spent the last three years of my life watching romantic movies or reading love stories."

"Oh, sweet Jesus. That's a lot of pressure if you're going to try to compare real life to fiction." He sucked in a deep breath. "You're so young. You have so much ahead of you."

"Are you saying you don't want to take me to bed?"

"Not even close." He kissed her nose. "Embarrassing question coming. Have you ever experienced sexual pleasure?"

Her face turned five different shades of red.

"I take it that's a no."

"Not with a man," she stammered. "But I... I... I've..." She covered her face with her hands.

Gently, he peeled her fingers back. "It's a good thing that you learned to give that to yourself. Every woman should."

"I was told it was against God."

"Let's leave your old church out of this conversation going forward." He helped her off the stool and guided her toward the master bedroom. "I want to do something for you—to you—that is only about you. It's part of sex, but not the act itself. Do you trust me?"

"Yes," she said.

He pushed open the door. His heart hammered in his chest like a teenage boy. Fear gripped his soul. He wanted to give her the kind of pleasure she deserved. He wanted to make her feel as if she were the most important person in his world. That her emotions were all that mattered.

"If at any time you feel uncomfortable or want me to stop, just tell me. This isn't about me or my needs. But yours."

"You must know that statement alone is strange to me."

"I'm sure it is, but believe me when I say that when two people are together, it's give and take. My turn will come in time."

"Okay."

Gently, he laid her on the mattress. Quickly, he removed his shirt. That would be the only article of clothing of his that he'd be shedding. He slid in next to her, running his hand up over her hip, squeezing gently. "All you need to do is relax, enjoy, and let me know what you like or don't like."

He raised her shirt, leaning over and kissing her taut stomach. Her chest rose with each choppy breath. Carefully, he lifted the flimsy fabric over her head, exposing her unsophisticated white bra. It wasn't a typical sexy undergarment, but it sent his senses into overdrive.

He rolled her yoga pants over her hips and down her legs.

Her breath hitched.

"Are you okay?"

"Yup," she said, staring at the ceiling, gripping the sheets.

His conscience tugged at his heart.

"Promise me you'll tell me if you—"

"I want to experience this, so please just stop asking me." She sat up and unhooked her bra, letting it fall to her waist. Quickly, she cupped her perfect round breasts.

He leaned in and kissed her neck, dotting more kisses, and moved down, pushing her hands away until he found her nipple, sucking it into his mouth.

Grabbing his head, she groaned.

That was a good sign.

He pinched and twisted the other one. She was so beautiful. And so sweet. She was like no one he'd ever met and he wanted desperately to hear his name rolling off her tongue in the throes of passion.

Pushing her back on the mattress, he removed the rest of her clothing, sliding his hand between her legs.

Immediately, she tensed and then relaxed as he dipped a finger inside while rolling her nipple around with his tongue.

He couldn't hold out. He needed to taste her. To savor her. He scooted to the edge of the bed, resting her legs over his shoulders.

"What are you doing?" She lifted her head and stared at him with wide eyes.

Could she actually be this naive?

"If you don't like this, I'll stop. But I believe you will."

She nodded.

He licked the inside of her thigh. Her gaze never left his and he realized she might not stop watching.

That was up to her.

He fingered her again and again. Then licked his fingers, getting a good taste. Jesus, she was delicious. It was like diving into his favorite desert, strawberries and whipped cream drizzled with chocolate.

He flicked his tongue over her hard nub.

"Oh my God." Her hips jerked upward and she clutched her breasts.

"Do you like that?"

"Yes," she said between pants. "Please don't stop."

That was all the encouragement he needed. He settled between her legs, doing his best to take things slow, but she wiggled against his mouth and moaned loudly.

Seconds later, her body quivered.

And quivered again.

Her thighs pinned his head for a long moment before she dropped them to the sides.

He palmed her, gauging whether or not she might be able to do that again. Sliding in two fingers, she rolled her hips against his hand.

She gripped his shoulders, tugging him closer.

He couldn't afford to get any closer or he might be tempted to do more. Instead, he flicked his tongue over her clit.

"Oh God. It's happening again," she whispered.

Music to his ears.

He slowed his motions, giving her a chance to catch her breath. He crawled back to the bed, pulling her close to his chest.

"I didn't know that existed." She nuzzled her face into his neck.

"Now that you do, you should never be deprived."

"But you are."

"Nope. If you're satisfied, I am too."

"I'm not so naive that I don't know when a man is in need of attention." She raised her hand.

He grabbed it before it got close to his waist. "We're not doing anything other than that today," he said. "Besides, we're supposed to be at the women's shelter in an hour. Time for showers. You can use the master. I'll take one in the guest room."

"I don't want to kick you—"

He hushed her with a kiss. "I insist." He lifted the blanket, covering her body. "We can stop at the restaurant and grab a breakfast sandwich." He stood.

"Phoenix?" She clutched the covers to her chin.

"Yes?"

"Thank you."

"You don't ever have to thank me for something as selfish as that."

She blushed. "I feel like the selfish one."

He leaned over and kissed her sweet lips. "Not even close." He turned and stepped from the master. He leaned against the door and closed his eyes. No one had ever touched his heart the way Janelle had. If he were being honest, she'd taken it and he was never getting it back.

8

"How are you doing?"

Janelle glanced up from her sandwich. "Would it be weird to say I'm doing great?"

Foster laughed. "No. Not at all." He pulled up a chair. "Some of my most rewarding days outside of being with my family are spent here at this shelter."

"What you all do here for these women and their children is amazing."

"I wish I could say that everyone who walks through these doors doesn't ever have to suffer heartbreak again. But unfortunately, it doesn't work that way. There are many who go back to their abusers or are taking drugs and can't kick the habit. My ex-wife was one of them."

"Phoenix told me what happened. I'm so sorry."

Foster nodded. "Thank you. I tried to help her as best I could. But she could never put herself or anyone else before the drugs. It caused our families a lot of pain. But I'm in a better place now. I found love again. I have a beautiful wife. A wonderful family. I'm happy."

"I'm glad."

He reached out and took her hand. "I've been watching you with the women and their kids here. You have a lot of compassion and a ton to offer. I hope you will consider being a regular face here."

"I plan on it."

"Good."

Phoenix came rushing through the doors. "We've got a situation," he said, wiping his brow. "Samatha's water just broke and I guess her contractions are right on top of each other. I called an ambulance, but she's in distress."

Janelle jumped to her feet. "I'm no midwife, but I have helped deliver at least fifteen babies."

"I can't say I've delivered any." Phoenix let out a long breath. "I've done and seen a lot of things, but childbirth isn't one of them."

"I was there my for kid's birth." Foster stood. "But Sam's six weeks early. And she's addicted to drugs. This might not go well."

"Where is she?" Janelle asked.

JEN TALTY

"In the main room. We have her over in the corner, but she's freaking out." Phoenix held the door open.

Janelle raced through the doors, dodging between people. She didn't have a clue about drugs. Or addiction. But she understood the fear of early labor, the feeling of being alone. She'd met Sam for a few moments. She was a single mother who had left her boyfriend, who was also her sex trafficker, a term that was new to Janelle, but it hadn't taken long for it to sink in what it meant.

She found Sam lying on a cot. Another one of the volunteers sat with her, holding her hand while she screamed out in pain.

"I feel it coming," Sam managed.

"The ambulance is ten minutes away," Phoenix said.

"Samatha, are you okay if I take a look and see what's going on?" Janelle asked.

Sam nodded.

As quickly as she could, Janelle examined Sam. The baby's head was right there. Janelle didn't have to do anything but peer under the sheet.

"Okay. I need some clean towels. Sterilized scissors. And everyone but Phoenix and Foster to go away."

"You want me here for this?" Phoenix asked with wide eyes.

She glared.

"Okay. You're the boss." He let out a long breath.

"Sam. Look at me." Janelle climbed onto the small cot. "Whether you're ready or not, this baby is. The next time you feel a contraction, I want you to push. Got it?"

Sam nodded.

"Foster. Your job is to sit by her head and encourage her. Phoenix, you're down here with me. Just do what I tell you to."

One of the volunteers handed her what she'd asked for.

"Oh God. Here we go." Sam gripped Foster's hand.

"Hold back her knees," Janelle said. "Bear down and push." She focused on the head, but it didn't move. She reached forward, pressing her hand on Sam's belly. "Come on, Sam. You've got this."

She groaned but stopped pushing and the head disappeared back in the birth canal.

"Next contraction, you need to push harder. I need you to give it all your might," Janelle said. "Foster, count to twenty with her, okay?"

"Got it," Foster said.

"If you can, get behind her and help pull her

knees closer to her chest. This baby keeps going back inside." Janelle had seen that a few times before. It wasn't uncommon. But it could be for other reasons, and that's what worried Janelle.

Sam's face turned red.

"Okay, here we go," Janelle said. The head appeared, coming out a little farther. This time, she saw the cord wrapped around the neck. "See that?" She glanced toward Phoenix.

"I honestly have no idea what I'm looking at." Phoenix snapped on a pair of gloves.

Janelle didn't want to scare Sam more than she already was.

"Sam, I need you to take a breath, okay? Next contraction, when you push, you're going to feel me help the baby out."

Sam sucked in a deep breath.

Janelle repositioned herself, handing the scissors to Phoenix. "The cord's wrapped around the baby's neck," she whispered. "I need you to cut it as I pull this kid out."

"You've got to be kidding me." He knelt next to her.

"Nope."

Sam growled.

Janelle did her best to curl her fingers around the baby's head. She felt the cord. It was tight. No way was this kid coming any farther. She managed to tuck her finger under the cord. "Do it now."

Phoenix reached in and snipped the cord.

"I need you to push again, Sam," Janelle said. "Come on. You got this. The head's out. We just got to move the shoulders." Tears filled Janelle's eyes. The baby was blue. Too blue. Her hands trembled as she took the baby into her arms and rubbed its back. "Come on, breathe for me, little girl. Breathe."

Her child never took a single breath. Never cried. Never had a chance.

The baby startled. A single faint cry.

"That's it," Janelle whispered.

"Is my baby okay?" Sam leaned forward, wiggling her fingers. "I want to hold my baby."

More faint cries.

Janelle placed the little girl on her mother's chest.

"The ambulance is here." Phoenix rested his hand on her shoulder.

She rocked back on her knees, letting out a long breath.

The paramedics raced to the bedside. "We'll take over now."

Janelle stepped aside. All the pain from her past left her in a flash. That little girl stood a chance now. Hopefully, Sam would get the help she needed.

Phoenix wrapped his strong arms around Janelle,

pressing his lips against her temple. "That was intense. And incredible. I don't know what would have happened had you not been here."

"The paramedics would have known what to do." She rested her head on his shoulder.

"But would they have gotten here in time?" He cupped her face. "You knew exactly what to do. You might have saved that little girl."

"He's right." One of the paramedics approached them. "That baby isn't completely out of the woods. But because of what you did during that delivery, she has half a chance. Are you a doctor? Nurse?"

"No," she said.

"Well, you'd make for a good one." The paramedic held out his hand. "Samatha would like to see you before we roll her and her baby away."

"Sure." Janelle slipped from Phoenix's embrace and made her way to the gurney. She took Sam's hand. "You did good, mama."

"I thought the world was punishing me for all the terrible things I did during this pregnancy. I figured for sure she was going to die because I was such a terrible mother."

"Don't ever speak like that." Janelle squeezed her hand. "God doesn't punish people that way. You have an opportunity to change your life right here. Right now." She waved her free hand. "Everyone here cares about what happens to you and this little angel. No one cares what you did yesterday. Only what you do going forward."

"Would it be okay with you if I named my little girl Janelle?"

"Oh my." Janelle placed her hand over her chest. "I'd be honored."

"Thank you for everything," Sam said.

"We better get going." The paramedic squeezed Janelle's shoulder. "We're also always looking for good people at our station if you ever want to go through the training." He smiled. "Take care."

Phoenix stood next to her, resting his hand on the small of her back. "Being a good Samaritan feels pretty damn spectacular, doesn't it?"

"I was so freaking scared when I saw that cord. I know what it's like to have a baby be born dead. That's all I could think about." She turned, throwing herself into his arms, and burst into tears.

"Oh, sweetheart." He held her so tight, running his hands up and down her back. "I'm so sorry that brought all that back up for you."

"Nope. I'm not going to do this." She sucked in a deep breath, taking a step back. "While that was one of the most painful things I've ever had to go through, deep down, if it hadn't happened, I wouldn't be here today. I wouldn't have found my freedom and I never want to feel trapped again."

"I'm in total awe of you. Of your strength. Your compassion. Your empathy. But mostly your ability to persevere under pressure. I'm a badass soldier and I was totally panicking out there. Watching you take charge like that, I can't help but want to shout from the rooftops, that's my girlfriend."

She cocked her head. "Girlfriend?"

"Too much of a commitment for you?"

"I think I'm the one who should be wondering if it's too much of one for you." She smiled. "Three people here have warned me that you're a bit of a player. Although, I'm not exactly sure what that means."

He laughed. "Come on, girlfriend. I'm taking you out to dinner."

"Not until I shower."

"Fair enough." He took her hand and led her to the main doors.

The second they stepped outside, someone with a camera shoved it in front of their faces.

She blinked.

"Are you the woman who delivered a baby a little while ago?" A female reporter shoved a microphone in her face. "Are you Janelle Kodi? Can you make a statement for us, please?"

"Not now." Phoenix pushed his hand up. "Give us some space."

"Samatha, the mother, stated that Janelle is a real hero. All we want is a few words," the reporter said.

"Leave us and the mother alone. There are other more important stories out there." Phoenix wrapped a protective arm around Janelle.

"Seriously, Phoenix." The woman lowered her arm. "Why are you cockblocking me? It's a great feel-good story. It's uplifting. My viewers will eat it up."

"Because all you want are ratings," he said.

"Of course that's part of it," the reporter said. "But this is one of those stories that makes the community come together. It erases all the bad shit. Come on. One statement."

"It's not up to me. It's up to Janelle." He turned. "Do you want to?"

"I'd rather not," she said.

"There you have it." Phoenix shrugged. "With that, we'll be on our way." He stepped around the reporter.

"Was that mean?" Janelle asked. She had no desire to be on camera. She understood there was local news and national news, but she didn't want to risk her face being plastered anywhere. It's why she never got on social media.

"Not at all. That reporter is a pain in the ass

anyway." He gripped her hand. "I was thinking instead of going out, we could hang at home. Eat pizza and watch a movie."

"And maybe some other stuff."

He paused midstep. "How about we sleep in the same bed and enjoy cuddling."

"What if I wanted more?"

"You might be able to twist my arm, but I don't want to rush things."

"Are you like this with all the women you date?"

"No," he said. "But no one has ever made me want to do it right before."

9

Phoenix flicked off the light in the master bathroom. This had been the first house he'd ever owned. It was the first place that felt like a home. A sanctuary. Since moving in, he'd never had a woman spend the night. He'd dated, sort of. But he always ended up going back to their places and often, he found reasons to leave. The older he got, the more he told himself that he enjoyed his space. That he preferred sleeping alone.

However, it had also become a lonely existence.

He couldn't admit that to anyone, not even his brothers or parents. He didn't know how to articulate it. Relationships had never been his thing. Being tied to any person—or even a place—had always made him jumpy. That was until his brothers had found Blue Moon.

That filled his heart with more joy than he knew what to do with. It had given him everything he thought he needed for the last few years. Only, an emptiness had crept into his soul and the moment he'd laid eyes on Janelle, he knew only one thing could fill that void.

Love.

What a foreign concept.

He stepped into the master bedroom, wearing a pair of pajama bottoms. Normally, he'd sleep in boxers or nothing, but he didn't think that would be appropriate, especially if he wanted to remain a gentleman.

His breath hitched when he saw Janelle sprawled in her modest nightgown in his king-sized bed. Who said a woman needed lingerie to be sexy?

"What do you want to watch?" She handed him the remote as he pulled back the covers.

"Whatever you want. Makes no difference to me."

"You have to have an opinion."

He hit the power button and the television roared to life. He tapped one of the streaming apps. "This show looks like it could be good."

"It is. I've seen it."

"What about this one?" He scrolled to one Brandi had recommended.

"Okay. I'm game." He hit play, then set the

remote on the nightstand, wrapping his arm around Janelle, waiting for all of this to become uncomfortable or weird.

But every bone in his body told him this was natural. Normal. As if this was the way his life should be.

Nelson had fallen in love with Brandi quickly. However, it had taken them a year to define their relationship and make it official.

Maverick and Hensley both had been hit with instant love, but Hensley fought it because she didn't believe she could give Maverick what he wanted most.

A family.

Until one dropped in their lap.

Phoenix had gone through life not wanting the entanglement of being responsible for someone else's feelings. That pressure was too much. Too intense.

In this moment, it's all he wanted. He wanted to protect and care for Janelle the way she deserved. He wanted to make her happy. To see her smile and to watch her eyes light up when she felt joy. The mere thought of her walking out of his life left him empty and cold.

Her fingers danced across the center of his chest and she wedged her knee between his legs.

Gently, he moved it away.

She shoved it back.

"Not a safe place to rest your leg." He lifted her hand and kissed the inside of her palm.

She snuggled in closer, locking her foot under his ankle.

He groaned. "Are you trying to be mean?"

Her hot lips pressed firmly against his shoulders and lingered way too long. She glanced up. Her lashes fluttered over her deep blue eyes.

"You're missing the show," he said.

Biting her lower lip, she pulled back the covers and straddled him. "What if I don't want to watch it?"

Gripping her thighs, he took in a slow breath through his nose, letting it out through his mouth. "It's going to be impossible for me to deny you anything you want."

"I want to be with you."

He cupped the back of her neck, drawing her close, kissing her sweet lips. If he said no, she would take it as a rejection. If he said yes, he worried she might not be ready.

But that was her decision to make, not his, and that was something he had to accept.

He gazed into her unwavering stare. "I want you too."

"Then why are you insistent on us—"

He pressed his finger against her lips. "I was only trying to be respectful of the world you came from and not rush into things. We have time. However, if this is what you want right now, I'm not going to say no because it's all I can think about anyway."

Her smile was as wide as could be. "Really?"

"You have no idea." He flipped her over on her back. "But you have to promise me you won't be submissive. That you will do your best to communicate your thoughts. Wants. Desires. Needs. I get that might not be easy. But being with me isn't a one-way street."

"You just rolled me over like I was a sack of potatoes." She smiled. Her eyes twinkled. "I'm not being submissive, but I didn't see that coming."

"Sorry. I got a little excited."

"I'm not complaining." She wrapped her legs around his waist. "I get the mechanics. I understand how the biology works. I'm not an idiot."

"Sweetheart, I never said you were." He took her mouth in a wet, wild, passionate kiss. He threw caution out the window. He needed to trust that she was capable of using her voice and that he was smart enough to know if she wasn't enjoying herself.

Or felt threatened in any way.

His pulse raged out of control. With every tender touch, his resolve to make things last as long as possible slipped through his fingers. Before he knew it, she was gloriously naked and his body throbbed and ached to fill every inch of her.

She slipped her hand into his pajamas.

He grabbed her wrist.

"Why are you stopping me? Am I doing something wrong?" she asked.

"Absolutely not," he whispered. "But you come first." He kissed his way down the center of her chest, rubbing his finger over her sensitive clit. It was warm and wet.

She withered under his touch, gripping at his shoulders, raising her hips, demanding more.

And he gave it to her.

Without hesitation or reservation.

Her climax came hot and fast, much like it had earlier. It humbled and excited him, leaving him breathless. If the night ended there, he'd be satisfied.

But it became apparent, she wouldn't have been.

It took a few moments for Janelle to catch her breath after her orgasm tore through her body. She blinked, staring at the ceiling fan. Phoenix had rocked her world for the third time that day in ways she'd never imagined.

And she desperately wanted to do the same for him.

He scooted up alongside her, rolling to his back.

She ran her hand up and down his stomach. With each pass, she moved closer to slipping her hand inside his pajama bottoms.

While she'd seen a man naked before, she'd never really experienced it. Touched it. Or wanted to. The male anatomy represented oppression. Domination. It was the thing that kept her from being free from having a voice.

But with Phoenix, his masculinity gave her power.

He batted her hand away.

"Why do you keep doing that?" She flicked her nail across his nipple.

He hissed. "I'm being shy."

"I doubt you've ever been shy in your life." She ran her finger across one of his many scars. So far, she'd counted seven. Bending over, she traced her tongue across the long one from his belly down to his hip. "What's this from?"

"It's the reason I was taken off active duty."

"What happened?"

"A piece of metal went through my body, breaking my hip."

"That sounds painful." She tugged at his bottoms.

"It wasn't fun, that's for sure." He tipped her chin

with his thumb. "I know you want to do for me what I did for you. But my body doesn't work the same way yours does. Once I'm done, I can't rebound and it's over. So, if I say you have to stop, I mean it. Otherwise, there will be no going further and I'm not sure that's what you want."

She chuckled.

"I'm glad you find that funny."

"What's hilarious is that you think I don't know that." She arched a brow. "I might not be experienced. And maybe I've never done certain things. But it doesn't mean I don't know about them."

He clasped his hands behind his head. "All right, then. Have your way with me."

She swallowed, trying to hide her shock. Teasing him came naturally, even if she wasn't used to the banter. However, she hadn't expected him to give her carte blanche with his body.

"Cat got your tongue?" he asked.

"Nope." Carefully, she eased him out of his pajamas. He was beautiful. Spectacular. Nothing like she'd remembered. The last time she'd seen a man, it had been a bit traumatizing.

But this? It was incredible. Empowering.

She touched. Stroked. Tasted.

He responded with soft moans. Gentle nudges. And the tensing of muscles.

"That's enough." He rolled her to her back and reached for something on the nightstand.

"What's that?"

"Protection."

"Excuse me?"

"A condom," he said.

"Oh. Birth control," she said. That would have been something she would have completely forgotten about and it did remind her of all the things in this world she didn't truly understand, even if she did. It was those little nuances of it all that passed her by.

He held her gaze, settling between her legs, entering her slowly.

It felt so different from what she remembered. With Jim, it had been rushed. Harsh. Sweaty. Gross.

This was a fairy tale. Phoenix stared into her eyes. He kissed her sweetly. He rocked in and out of her like a waltz. It was as if they fit together like the last piece of a puzzle.

And the buildup.

Holy shit. She thought she was going to explode.

Which she did.

Her climax hit hard and fast. It rocked her so intensely she cried out his name and dug her nails into his back, arching her hips high. Her lungs burned and she couldn't catch her breath. The moment she thought she could, another orgasm flew through her system.

And then his orgasm clashed with her third.

For a long time, she lay there, staring at the ceiling, unable to move, much less catch her breath.

He rolled to the side, pulling the covers over their bodies.

"Oh my God," she managed. "I had no idea it could be like that."

"Neither did I." He kissed her shoulder.

"Don't joke with me."

"I'm not." He tilted her chin with his finger. "I won't lie to you. I've been with a few women in my day. I'm not proud of that. But I'm not ashamed either. However, no one has mattered to me as much as you have and I can't explain right now in words what I'm feeling except to say I care very deeply for you."

"You don't have to say—"

He hushed her by pressing his lips over her mouth. "I know I don't have to say anything. I'm telling you how I feel because I want to."

She snuggled in close, wrapping her arms and legs around his body. "I care about you too." She let out a long sigh. "I don't know that I've ever cared about anyone like this."

"Same goes for me." He kissed her temple. "We

should get some sleep. We both have to work in the morning."

"Good night, boyfriend."

He chuckled. "I like the sound of that."

"It does have a nice ring to it." She closed her eyes and felt a great sense of belonging for the first time in her life.

10

"You've got an extra spring in your step this morning."

Phoenix tried to rein in his smile but gave up. He shrugged. "It's a beautiful day."

Nelson laughed. "I'd really like to know what put that grin on your face."

"I have my suspicions." Maverick leaned against the bar. "I believe her name's Janelle and she's got one to match."

"Fuck off." Phoenix lifted his soda and chugged, wishing it was closer to five so he could justify having a beer. "And don't you dare razz her."

"Wouldn't dream of it." Nelson raised his hands.

"I hate to be the one to bring this up, but did you see the news this morning?" Maverick asked.

"Unfortunately, we saw it." Last night had been

the best evening of Phoenix's life. He couldn't recall when he'd ever felt so alive. When he'd woken up with Janelle in his arms, he knew that's what he wanted for the rest of his life.

And not in a generic way.

But with her.

"I can't believe Gina did that, after you asked her not to," Maverick said. "She not only gave Janelle's name, but also showed a picture of you and her together."

"Gina's only after headlines and ratings and she got them with that story." Phoenix didn't think anything could sour his mood, but that certainly was a killjoy. "Janelle wasn't happy."

"Can't say as I blame her." Nelson took an order from one of the waitresses and filled it. "That poor girl has been through it and then some. But she doesn't have anything to fear."

"Sure, she does." Phoenix let out a long breath. "The more Mom has uncovered about that cult, the more dangerous I believe they are. If her dad ever finds out where she is, I'm sure he'll do whatever is in his power to make sure his daughter returns."

"As long as she's here, Adam Weiss is going to have to go through all of us to get to her." Maverick squeezed Phoenix's shoulder.

"I appreciate the support," Phoenix said.

"Has she given any more thought into going public with her story? Or pressing charges against her dad and spiritual husband or whatever the hell he's called?" Nelson asked.

"We had a brief discussion about it on our way to work, but she cut me short. She didn't want to ruin how things have been going with such a heavy topic." Phoenix could understand where Janelle was coming from. Her reactions to what had happened at the women's shelter and her own plight were in conflict. She could do good and help people, while walking away from a destructive past.

She couldn't save everyone.

No one could.

It also wasn't her responsibility.

He couldn't fault her for wanting some peace in her life.

"Have you told her about everything that Mom dug up?" Maverick asked.

"I mentioned it, but I haven't shown her the documents." Phoenix's heart tightened. He didn't like keeping this from Janelle and he knew he ran the risk of pissing her off, but so far, the intel had been incomplete. "Mom was having a conference call with her friend today. I should know more later and I'll talk with Janelle tonight."

"Take it from me, you don't want to keep that from her too long." Nelson arched a brow.

"I don't want to upset her with partial information. She's annoyed enough as it is about having her face shown on a local news program." Phoenix nodded in the direction of one of the regulars as they waved and headed out the door. "Unfortunately, that's the kind of feel-good story that could get picked up on a national level and even though there aren't televisions or papers in the compound where she lived, it doesn't mean the elders of her church wouldn't see it."

Nelson and Maverick exchanged a glance.

"What aren't the two of you telling me?" Phoenix polished off the rest of his soda.

"Pam's making a bit of a stink about what happened yesterday," Nelson said. "One of the waitresses who is friendly with Pam mentioned she's been going around telling anyone who will listen that what Janelle did was reckless. That she could have done more damage by the way she delivered that baby because she has no medical training."

"I don't give a shit what Pam thinks." Phoenix wiped down the bar with a towel.

"You might want to because Pam plans on doing an interview with Gina," Maverick said.

"Why the fuck would Gina interview her?" Phoenix asked.

"According to the gossip around this bar, she's looking to chat with anyone who knows Janelle since Janelle has refused to comment," Maverick said.

"That's just fucked up." Phoenix sighed. "Why can't people just do a good deed and be left alone."

"Gina's making a big deal about the fact that Samatha chose to name her baby after Janelle. She went on record saying that Janelle not only saved her child, but has also made her want to change her life. That Janelle is an inspiration to all women like Samatha." Nelson hopped from the bar stool. "I take it Janelle shared some of her past with the women at the shelter."

"She related to them," Phoenix said. "She was empathic. She listened to them and didn't judge them, but she didn't get into her life story. That said, she did spend time alone with Samatha and few other women. I honestly have no idea if she got into any detail. But I doubt it. Janelle isn't ready. She hasn't had therapy and that girl has been through some serious trauma."

"It amazes me how well adjusted she is for someone who fled a cult three years ago and has been on her own ever since." Nelson tapped his fingers on the counter. "That takes some serious balls."

"She's a fighter, that's for sure," Phoenix said. "She's an old soul in so many ways. But incredibly naive about too many things in the real world still. There's a part of her that wants to come forward and tell her story. She carries so much guilt for leaving behind others like her who are suffering in silence. But she's also aware enough about her own plight that she's not prepared to take on her father and his church."

"She might not ever have to. That church could blow up all on its own." Maverick pointed to the door. "Mom's here and she looks a bit frazzled. Like she used to when she was working a big case."

"Retirement was hard on her," Nelson said.

"She's always asking Hensley if she can help out." Maverick shook his head. "So's Dad. They both say they are enjoying their golden years, but the reality is they miss working."

"They're both in their sixties. They need to slow down and smell the roses." Nelson laughed. "When they aren't spending time with the grandkids, they're looking for shit to do. I wish they could do some front porch sitting. It's good for the soul."

"They'll get there." Phoenix smiled. "Hey, Mom. What's going on? I didn't expect to see you here this morning. Aren't you supposed to be helping Hensley with the kids today?"

"Dad's handling those two little monsters." She held up her briefcase. "I need to talk to you. Get me a cup of coffee, get Janelle, and let's go to your office."

"Maybe you and I should chat first before bringing Janelle in," Phoenix said.

His mom tilted her head and narrowed her stare.

He swallowed. He hated that look. It was the same look she'd given him when he'd given her a hard time as a teenager, and he knew he was about to get grounded. There was no coming back when his mother held his gaze like that.

"You've gotten serious with this girl, and don't try to tell me you haven't." His mom lowered her chin, daring him to argue.

"How can I be serious with a woman I've only known a few weeks?" he asked.

Both his brothers snickered.

"The peanut gallery can shut the hell up and leave," he said.

"Come on, man." Maverick reached over the bar and slapped him on the shoulder. "I've been there. I fell hard and fast and I'm enjoying watching it happen to you. We all like Janelle. She's good for you."

"I never thought I'd see my little brother in love." Nelson waggled his brows. "You've done your best to avoid it and now it's hit you like a freight train."

"You all toss that word around like it's fact." Phoenix had been grappling with his emotions for the last week. They had crept into his heart, captured it, and they weren't going to release it. This morning, when he opened the truck door to help her into the passenger side, he gazed into her eyes and that single word hung in his brain like a brick.

He couldn't say it because it was insane.

It wasn't the baggage that she brought to the table. He could handle that. Everyone had a past, including him. Hers was no longer an issue. He'd obviously gotten over that hang-up, and so had she.

"Because it is," his mother said. "All you have to do is admit it to yourself and then to her. It's that easy."

"Nothing is easy about this situation." He folded his arms across his chest.

Mistake.

His mother grabbed his wrist and yanked. "Don't get all closed off with me. Or try to use what's happening around this poor girl as an excuse to mask your feelings."

"Jesus, Mom. That's not what I'm doing," he said. "All I meant was that things are complicated and I'm not willing to toss around a word that has a big meaning so soon."

"That's a cop-out, little brother," Nelson said. "I have work to do." He kissed his mother's cheek.

"I agree with Nelson." Maverick did the same. "I'll be around if you need me." He left Phoenix alone with their mother.

Her face softened. "All I want for you is to be happy and this last year you haven't been until that girl walked into your life."

"That's not entirely true."

"But it's not false," she said. "You've been lost. I've been watching how you are with your brothers and their families. Both your father and I saw the conflict in your eyes." She rested her hand over his. "Of all our boys, you took to military life the best. It was your calling. More so than Nelson and Maverick."

"Mom, all of us loved our careers."

"I know that. But Nelson and Maverick always wanted more out of life. They wanted marriage and kids. That never crossed your mind when you were enlisted. As parents, we accepted that you might be the kid who never gave us grandkids. But when you were injured, your world changed."

"I don't need reminding of that." He rubbed his hip. The limp was long gone, but the dull ache had never subsided. He lived with pain every day of his life. A constant reminder of what had been taken from him long before he'd been ready. "I remember all too well lying in that hospital bed, being told my active duty days were over. I resigned myself to a desk job. I accepted my fate."

"Until your brothers gave you a way out. You jumped on that chance so fast and not just because that was a dream you shared with Maverick and Nelson, but because that position in the Army wasn't fulfilling." She held up her hand. "Since then, you've gone from one woman who was incapable of giving you love to the next."

"Are you suggesting my taste in girls has always been horrible?" This wasn't the first time he'd had this conversation with his mother, but it was the first time she'd gone this deep, and he found himself wanting to hear her point of view.

"They were all nice ladies, but they were all ships passing in the night. They were like you. Lost souls, going from port to port, not sure of what they wanted or what to look for. When Janelle landed in Lake George, she was looking for a place to land. A place to call home. A safe haven. She found it in you. She might not have been looking for love, but that's the door she knocked on and you answered."

"I'll admit that I care about her more than anyone I've ever dated. But love is too strong a word."

"And I call bullshit. You're just scared."

He raked his fingers through his hair. "Of what?"

"Pardon the bad comparison, but of being put on a desk job." She arched a brow.

"What the hell does that mean?"

"Janelle's life might have been sheltered. She doesn't have a lot of real-world experiences. However, she has lived through some shit and when she comes out on the other end, and she will, she's going to be stronger. She's already showing that in the few weeks she's been here. You're afraid that she's going to see what this world can offer and it's not going to be you, just like you moved past that desk job."

Sometimes he resented how insightful his mother could be and right now, he wished he'd never asked because it made too much damn sense. He'd never looked at it that way.

He opened his mouth, but no words formed.

"Life is full of risks, son. You've never taken one with your heart." She squeezed his hand. "Janelle is worth taking it. I wouldn't say that if I didn't believe it."

"That's a lot to digest," he whispered.

"I'm sure it is. I'll leave it alone for now." She smiled. "I do have some things to chat about and I really do want Janelle there."

"I'd rather spoon-feed the intel."

His mother shook her head. "You can't keep

things from her, and I need to know if she recognizes some people."

"All right. I'll go get her and a pot of coffee. Go make yourself comfortable in the office." He slipped from behind the bar with his heart beating in his throat. All he wanted to do was protect Janelle, but his mother had a point. Knowledge was power and Janelle needed both.

"Hi, Mrs. Snow." Janelle strolled into the office. "How are you this afternoon?"

"I'm good, dear, but how many times do I have to tell you to call me Dina?"

Janelle smiled. "Dina," she said. "I'll work on that."

Dina laughed. "You do that because Mrs. Snow, may she rest in peace, was my mother-in-law and she was a pain in my ass."

Phoenix laughed. "Grammy wasn't that bad."

Dina sat in the chair in front of the computer and lowered her chin. "Your grammy was a mean old bird who never liked me. She thought a woman's place was in the kitchen. She hated that I worked and thought I was a horrible mother. Every time you boys acted out or got into trouble, it was all my fault. I'll never forget when you got yourself suspended from school." Dina smacked her forehead. "That woman came right over to the house and scolded me. Not you. She told me that if I had been home, doing my job, you wouldn't have even thought to get into a fight. She never once asked what the fight was about."

Janelle eased onto the sofa, totally fascinated by the story. She glanced up at Phoenix, who leaned against the doorjamb with a wicked grin and a mischievous twinkle. "You got suspended from school? How old were you?"

"That time? I was thirteen," he said.

"It happened more than once?" she asked.

"That little devil got suspended three times. All for the same thing. Fighting. While I never condone throwing punches, Phoenix didn't toss the first one." Dina laughed. "Grammy was fit to be tied, but again, it wasn't about the fight, but about the fact I worked."

"I get the connection, because in the world I grew up in, women weren't allowed to work. It was our job to raise children and to do it right. Living out here in the real world, I get that's kind of dumb and I've seen all sorts of women do it alone and the kids are fine," Janelle said. "But I have to ask, what was the fight about?"

Dina smiled as if she were proud. "Like I said, I

don't agree with fighting, but when my kid over there is defending a girl's honor after another boy pulled down her pants in the hallway, he can get suspended all he wants. That other kid deserved something."

Janelle glanced between Dina and Phoenix. "That's so mean what that boy did. What happened to him?"

"He was expelled from school," Phoenix said. "So he got his punishment, but according to everyone, I shouldn't have broken his nose."

Janelle covered her mouth and laughed. "I'm sorry, that's not funny."

"Actually, it is," Dina said. "Every fight Phoenix got suspended for was because he was sticking up for some kid who was being bullied by someone else. But all my mother-in-law could see was that I wasn't home when the boys got off the bus, so she blamed me. She used to tell the boys' father that he needed to have a firmer hand with his wife."

Janelle cringed, recoiling in the sofa.

"Oh, honey. She didn't mean hit me," Dina said. "She only meant that if he were more of a man, he'd be able to control me and make me stay at home."

"A firm hand means something different in the compound. It's what husbands do when one of their wives steps out of line or isn't obedient and it always involves physical punishment." It amazed Janelle how open she'd become about her past with everyone in the Snow family. They never showed her judgment. Only love and support.

Not that she'd ever told anyone other than Jason, Anne Marie, and the few people at the first place she stayed while she got a high school diploma and learned a few skills so she could make it in the real world.

Outside of that, she kept her head down and never breathed a word of her past to anyone.

"My grammy had strong, old-fashioned opinions. My father didn't believe in them and it caused a few rifts in the family," Phoenix said. "I'm sorry that those things happened to you."

"We're grateful that you got out and found your way to us." Dina pulled out a file from her briefcase. "Things are starting to crumble for your father's church." She handed the folder to Phoenix. "But there still isn't enough to grant the Feds a search warrant for the compound. They are working with this couple who have helped a few people escape. This couple won't give names, but they have told their stories. They didn't leave the same church, but it's a similar tale."

Janelle swallowed. "What are the couple's names?"

"Jason and Anne Marie Wilcox," Dina said.

All the air in Janelle's lungs flew out like a bird

taking flight. She gripped the cushion and tried to breathe normally, but it felt as though her heart had stopped beating.

Phoenix rushed to her side. He set the folder on the coffee table and took her hands. "I take it you know these people."

She nodded. "Anne Marie is who I met when I lost my baby. She's the one who planted the seed that I could leave if I wanted to. It took three months before I made that call, but she and Jason got me out. They helped me with a new name. My GED. They gave me some money. Got me a car and sent me on my way."

"They're good people," Dina said. "But they are being pressured to help find someone who will tell their story and press charges against someone in that church. Without that, the Feds can't do anything."

"When I left the safe house, they told me to go buy a phone. They didn't want the number. They didn't want to be able to contact me or know how to reach me. All they know is my name," she said. "I do have their number, if I wanted to contact them."

"Your name is enough to find you." Dina inched closer. "But they have made it clear to the FBI and local authorities that they won't give up the names of anyone they have helped." Dina held her gaze. "However, your father and so-called husband made an interesting statement this morning." She reached for the file, rifled through it, and handed her a piece of paper.

Phoenix took it before she had a chance to snag it in her shaky fingers.

"You've got to be fucking kidding me." Phoenix bolted off the couch. "This is not good."

"What does that say?" Janelle asked.

Phoenix handed her the document. "Your dad and Jim have reported Sister Aura Margret Bueller as missing. They have accused Jason and Anne Marie of kidnapping you."

"What? Why would they do that after I've been gone for three years?" Janelle stared at the piece of paper, but none of the words came into focus. "That doesn't make any sense."

"It gets worse," Dina said. "Your dad is saying you've only been gone for two days."

Janelle dropped the document. She stared at Dina, then shifted her gaze to Phoenix. "This is crazy."

"Here's the kicker." Dina came closer, taking her hands. "The church has footage of you being taken and Anne Marie and Jason have been brought in for questioning."

"No. No way. I know the compound has cameras, but if there are any images of me leaving, it's me using the keys I stole from my dad. I walked through the gate and I got into that car. Anne Marie and Jason didn't take me. They didn't even touch me."

"That's not the spin that the church is putting on this and right now, the evidence is pretty damning against Jason and Anne Marie with regard to you," Dina said. "The Feds have no choice but to look into it and there's only one way to put an end to it."

"That's one big fucking ask, Mom." Phoenix planted his hands on his hips and glared. "You should have come to me in private first. This is too much to toss at Janelle. She's never wanted to be the one to come forward and this puts her in a dangerous situation. They want her to come out of hiding so they can suck her right back in. They want that power back and they know the right buttons to push. You can't ask her to do this."

"I can speak for myself." Janelle ran her hands up and down her thighs. A million things ran through her brain. Images of her siblings. Her sister wives. All the children. All the innocent people that lived in that compound who didn't know any better and were being controlled. It had to stop and she had to the power to end it. "My dad and Brother Jim think of me as a weak woman. They still see me as the same girl who ran three years ago. They believe that I will, for whatever reason, hold on to the covenants of the church. Or that I will fear them so badly that once I see them, I will cower and be under their control and walk right back into my role. I've seen that before. Girls who've escaped and been brought back. Well, it's not going to happen with me." She stood tall, squaring her shoulders. "I'm going to give that interview with Gina. And I'm going to tell my story. All of it." She sucked in a deep breath. For the first time in her life, she held all the power. All the cards were in her hands. She was going to face the storm. No, she was going to run right into the storm.

She turned her attention to Phoenix. "While I'd like you at my side, I don't need your fists defending my honor. This is something I need to do. I'll never truly be free unless I totally stand up for myself and every woman and child who has had to live in my shoes." A single tear dribbled down her cheek.

Phoenix strolled across the room. He wiped it away, cupping her face. "Are you sure this is what you want to do?"

"Yes."

"Then I will support you all the way." He brushed his mouth tenderly across her lips.

"We all will," Dina whispered. "I'll give the two of you a moment." She slipped out the door, closing it behind her.

"That was quite the speech." Phoenix wrapped his

arms around her, holding her close. "I'm not sure if I'm insanely proud or utterly terrified of your newfound independence."

She dropped her head to his chest. "I'm scared to death to tell the world what happened to me. To open myself up to judgment and ridicule for staying. For leaving and not pressing charges earlier. It's very scary."

"You're not alone." He lifted her chin with his thumb. "You have a lot of people here who love and care about you."

Love.

That was an interesting word. Growing up, love was conditional. If she was a good girl and was obedient, she was loved. But if she dared to question, love was taken away.

She understood what it meant to care for someone and what it felt like to be cared for. She'd experienced that along the way. But she'd never formed true connections or been anywhere that she wanted to stay.

Until now.

"I owe you everything," she whispered. "You've shown me what life is all about. I don't know if I couldn't have gotten to a place where I would have found the strength to do this without you."

"I don't believe that." He kissed her nose. "Besides, you've given me something too."

"What's that?"

"If I tell you, I'll probably scare you away. It's been hard for me to admit for so many reasons that seem foolish now, but Janelle Kodi, you've stolen my heart and I don't want it back." He kissed her, hard, and with intent. It was wild. Passionate.

She gripped his shoulders while the room around her spun out of control. The love that crossed through her veins burst into flames.

But she wanted more.

She needed more.

Demanded all of it.

Breaking off the kiss, she palmed his cheek. "This might sound silly to you, but I've never heard the words before. And if you mean them, can you say them?"

"I do mean them, so yes, I can give them to you." He gazed into her eyes with adoring admiration. "I love you."

11

Phoenix clicked off the television. "So, how do you feel about that?"

"I don't know what was more emotional. Giving the interview or watching it on the TV." Janelle swiped at her cheeks. "The hardest part, honestly, was having to repeat all of it to the FBI and to the cops. That wasn't easy. Their questions were tough and not always kind."

"I'm sure it was, and I'm sorry I couldn't sit in with you on that." He took her hand and kissed her palm. The last week had been grueling to say the least.

Janelle had not only given an interview to Gina regarding delivering Samatha's baby, but also went on national television and told her story to the world, debunking her father's accusations.

"I feel so bad for all the women and children being displaced. It's going to be hard for them. This world is so foreign. It took me a long time to get used to it. I still struggle sometimes, and some of those people still believe in the doctrine. They will be susceptible to other people like my dad and Brother Jim."

"Unfortunately, there will always be people like them in this world. But what you did has brought major awareness to what goes on behind those compounds' walls. It's made it easier for the FBI to help women like you." He leaned forward and lifted his wineglass. "Thanks to you, Jason and Anne Marie are free to continue their work."

"You're making me out to be some kind of hero."

"Because you are." He polished off the glass. "Come on. Let's go to bed. We both have to be at the restaurant early." He took her hand and gave her a little tug.

"You know, I've been sleeping in your bed every night. People are going to start thinking we live together or something."

"Would that be so bad?"

"Are you asking me to move in with you?"

"You're the one who brought it up." He laughed, shrugging his shoulders. "But since we're on the topic, I would love it if you never left. I mean, I'd be lonely in that bed all by myself and this house would be empty and depressing without you."

"Okay, if you insist, I'll bring the rest of my stuff over."

"That was easy." His phone buzzed in his back pocket. He pulled it out and stared at the screen. "Fuck," he mumbled.

"What is it?"

"We have a big problem." Quickly, he sent a text message to his brothers, his parents, and to Stacey.

"Please don't leave me in the dark." She raised up on tiptoe, trying to get a look at his screen.

He took her by the shoulders. "I need you to go to the bedroom and stay there." Patting her bottom, he raced to the cabinet where he kept his weapon.

"Phoenix, you're scaring me and I need you to talk to me." She stood right behind him with her hand on his hip.

"Your father's lurking around the property."

"I thought he was in jail," she said with a shaky voice.

"So did I." He turned. "Please. I need you to go—"

"No. There's a big sliding glass door in there. I'm not leaving your side."

He sucked in a deep breath, letting it out slowly. "All right. But you have to promise me you'll do exactly what I say. I don't know if he has people with him or not. I only saw one person on the security camera. My mom has access to my system. She'll be my eyes and ears. Maverick is on his way. Nelson was at Blue Moon, but he's headed here and will be here as soon as he can. I also informed Stacey of the situation."

"I guess this is your area of expertise, so—"

Ding-dong.

"Really? He's going to come to my fucking front door?" Phoenix tucked his weapon in his belt. "Let me do the talking."

"That might be hard."

Phoenix laughed. "I really do like this side of you."

Janelle stood behind Phoenix as he opened the front door. She gripped his hips and peered around his massive shoulders.

Coming face-to-face with her father wasn't something she expected she'd have to do until the trial. If there was one. Rumor had it he might plea it out.

"May I help you?" Phoenix asked.

"Let's not pretend that you don't know who I am," her dad said. "May I come in?"

"No." Phoenix crossed his arms. "You're not welcome in our home."

"Our? My daughter is living here? In sin?" Her dad lifted his chin. "Tsk-tsk. You really are going to hell, Sister Aura."

"Don't call me that. My name's Janelle."

"You can change your name out here in this godforsaken place, but you are and will always be my daughter. Now let me in. We have some things to discuss." Her father took one step.

Phoenix pulled out his weapon, but he didn't aim it anywhere. Just made it known he had a gun. "I doubt you're supposed to be outside the state of New Mexico. Be warned, I've called the police. Now, please leave."

"I'd put that thing away if I were you, son." Her dad smiled that evil grin when he had something up his sleeve to get what he wanted.

"I'm not your son, so fuck off." Phoenix inched closer, puffing out his chest. "I'm not the kind of man you want to mess with. I served in the Army. Special Forces. I could kill you with my pinky if I wanted to."

"I'm not afraid of you and I'm certainly ready to meet my maker when the time comes." Her dad leaned closer. "But today is not that day." He held up his cell. "Bring the car forward."

Headlights appeared. "I do my homework and I

know what kind of man you are. You'll do anything for a damsel in distress. I've read that about you. So, you're not going to let anything happen to the two girls in the back seat of that vehicle."

"Who did you take? Who are you holding hostage?" Janelle tried to step around Phoenix, but he held out his arm.

Her father laughed. "You should be careful who you talk to, young lady."

The driver of the vehicle opened the passenger door and yanked Gina from the back seat. Her hands were tied behind her back, her mouth covered with duct tape.

Then came Pam.

Same thing.

Janelle gasped. "You bastard. They haven't done anything to you."

"That reporter has," her father said. "She helped spread lies about me. She poisoned my own daughter against me." He shrugged. "And the other one. Well, she wanted to hurt him—and you—and told me all sorts of lovely information. She's collateral damage."

"You're a stupid man," Phoenix said. "Like I said, I'm not the guy to fuck with. And you won't get away with this."

"But I already have," her father said. "Now, this is

how things will go down. I'll let those two walk away if you'll hand over my daughter. It's that simple."

"Not going to happen," Phoenix said, slamming the door shut.

"Why the hell did you do that?" Janelle glared. "Pissing him off is going to make those two women pay in ways I'm not willing to let them."

"Trust me." He squeezed her shoulder. "This will all be over in a matter of minutes."

Janelle wasn't so sure.

Phoenix lifted his cell and read the texts from his family. "Your father has four men surrounding the house. My brothers are working on quietly taking them out. I need to wait for word that they've done that before we act, but I also need to give them a little time to do that."

Janelle continued to glare at him as if she wanted to punch him in the throat. "My father is probably having his goon beat the crap out of those girls as we speak."

"I'm not going to let anything happen to them."

Pop!

Janelle jumped. "What was that?"

Shit. Nothing good. Phoenix pushed her out of

the way and opened the door, holding his weapon at the ready.

Adam still stood in the doorway. "You shouldn't have done that." He waved a gun. "The next time I shoot, I will kill someone."

Phoenix glanced toward the vehicle. Pam hunched over the hood. Blood trickled down her shirt. He narrowed his stare.

Flesh wound. Nothing serious.

"That won't be good for you. It will only add more time on your prison sentence," Phoenix said. A shadow off to the right caught his eye.

Maverick. He knew that crawl anywhere.

"I won't be going to prison because my daughter is going to tell the world it was all a lie. That she was forced to tell it by you."

"That's funny," Phoenix said.

Janelle inched closer, grabbing his arm. "I won't ever recant my story and if you hurt either one of those girls, I'll make sure you pay."

"I can sort of understand why you'd feel that way about the reporter. She had nothing but nice things to say about you. But the other one." Adam shook his head. "She hates you."

Phoenix's phone dinged.

That was his cue.

A red light flashed in the distance.

Phoenix let out a sigh of relief, only it didn't last long when Adam raised his weapon and pointed it directly at Janelle.

He stepped in front of her.

"One bullet, two birds." Adam smiled.

Phoenix shoved Janelle to the ground.

Bang!

Bang!

Adam's eyes grew wide. He lowered his gaze, clutching his chest. "You shot me," he whispered as he crumpled to the stoop.

"Damn fucking right I did." Phoenix grabbed the doorjamb. His lungs burned as he struggled for air. No matter how hard he tried, he couldn't catch his breath. "Motherfucker." God, he hated getting shot. He leaned against the wood frame and blinked.

"Phoenix!" Janelle pressed her hand on the wound.

"Shit, that hurts."

"Sorry." She let up.

He grabbed her hand and pushed it as hard as he could. Blood trickled between their fingers. "No. That's the right thing to do." Slowly, his legs gave way and he found himself on his ass, staring up at both his brothers and his mother.

"Paramedics are on their way," his mother said. "Let me take a look."

Janelle moved to the side.

"Don't leave me," he whispered.

"I'm not going anywhere." She held his gaze.

"Bullet didn't come out the back," his mother said. "He's losing a lot of blood. Where the fuck is the ambulance?"

"I love you, Janelle." Phoenix gazed into her eyes and the world faded to black.

12

Janelle paced in the waiting room of the hospital. It had been ten hours since they'd brought Phoenix in and eight hours since he'd gone to surgery.

"Honey, you should sit down and eat something." Dina waved her hand over all the food that Jack had brought from the restaurant.

"I'm not hungry." Janelle plopped herself into one of the chairs.

Her father was dead.

Brother Jim was in jail and going to prison for a long time since he was one of the men caught surrounding Phoenix's home and part of the kidnapping of Pam and Gina.

That part of her life was truly over.

But her future was fighting for his life.

The sliding doors opened, and she jumped to her feet, but it was only Pam.

"Any word yet?" Pam asked with her arm in a sling.

"Nothing." Janelle sighed. She wanted to hate Pam for bringing her dad to Phoenix's doorstep, but she couldn't. "How's your shoulder?"

"It's nothing for anyone here to worry about." Pam wiped a tear away. "I'm so sorry for what I've done. I know that's not enough, but—"

"I forgive you," Janelle said.

"We all do." Maverick nodded. "We appreciate your statement to the police and for at least trying to be a blood donor."

"I gave anyway. Maybe it will help someone else." Pam nodded. "I best be going, but please let me know how things turn out." She disappeared out the exit doors.

"Hopefully that girl has turned over a new leaf," Louis said.

Janelle snagged a fry and dunked it in ketchup. Her stomach defied her and growled.

"Here comes the doctor." Dina was on her feet in a flash. "How's my son doing?"

The doctor laughed. "He's awake and feeling fine.

As in the anesthesia is having quite the effect on him."

"How'd the surgery go?" Louis asked.

"He's a lucky man with nine lives, that's for sure." The doctor nodded. "The bullet didn't do any major damage, other than to his lung. That will repair in time. He'll have to stay here for a few days while that works itself out. He's on oxygen and he's pretty proud of the new scar he has where we went in to remove the bullet. Outside of that, he'll be as good as new in about four weeks."

Janelle covered her face and began to weep.

Louis wrapped a strong arm around her shoulders.

"He took that bullet for me. It should have been—"

"Stop that. And don't ever let him hear you talk like that either," Louis said. "We'd all walk into fire for each other." He pried her fingers from her cheeks. "You included. And when I say that, I mean you'd do the same for any one of us. We're family. That's what family does."

"Speaking of family. He keeps asking for Janelle. The love of his life. The prettiest woman who ever lived. The woman he's going to marry and grow old with," the doctor said.

Everyone in the waiting room burst out laughing.

Except Janelle.

She stood there, staring at the doctor, unable to move or say a single word.

"Cat got your tongue, young lady?" Louis nudged her with his hip.

"A little bit," she managed. "He's just drugged up and doesn't know what he's saying."

"We all know he's madly in love with you," Louis whispered. "I couldn't ask for a better daughter-in-law than you or the two I already have."

She blinked. "You people are crazy."

"Crazy in love with you, just like our son." Dina squeezed her arm. "Can we go see him?"

"Of course," the doctor said.

"I think you all should go first." Janelle wiped the tears from her face.

"Nope. That honor goes to the woman our brother loves." Maverick came up behind her and gave her a little shove.

"You're stuck with us now." Nelson laughed. "All of us. We're a package deal."

A smile slowly spread across her face. "There are worse things I can think of than that."

Phoenix waved his hand in front of his face. "When am I going to stop seeing double?"

The nurse chuckled. "It's going to be a bit," she said.

"Where's my family? Janelle?"

"The doctor went to go... Oh, here comes one of them." The nurse pulled back the curtain.

Phoenix smiled. "I've been waiting forever for you. I told you she was gorgeous. Isn't she the prettiest woman you've ever seen?"

"He's pretty loopy but incredibly coherent, considering." The nurse disappeared behind the ugly green and blue drapes.

"Come here." He patted the side of the bed.

"You gave everyone quite the scare." Janelle took his hand and eased onto the side of the bed.

"How about a kiss?"

She rolled her eyes but leaned forward and planted her sweet lips on his.

"Now that's what the doctor ordered."

"You're as high as a kite."

"Maybe a little, but I know what I'm saying." He took her hand and rested it against the good side of his chest. "When I woke up, all I wanted was to see you, because the last thing I remember was figuring I wasn't going to make it. But the doctors say I'm going to live to be an old man."

"You are an old man." She laughed.

He narrowed his stare. "That's mean, and no way to talk to your fiancé."

"That's presumptuous."

"That's a big word and I doubt in my current state I could even pronounce it."

"I wish I had my cell so I could video this. You're funny." She palmed his cheek. "That anesthesia has you talking crazy."

"Saying I love you isn't nuts."

"No, but the other stuff is."

He shook his head. He might be feeling the effects, but he was well aware of what he was doing. He sort of felt a little bad about pulling his family in on it. And he might regret it because he did struggle to put words together, but he knew what he wanted.

"How can wanting to spend the rest of my life with the woman I love be off the wall?" He pointed to the table by his bed. "Can you hand me that box?"

"Sure." She reached for it and placed it in his hand.

"Can you help me open it?"

"Of course." She lifted the lid and gasped. "Oh my God. Phoenix Louis Snow. What the hell is this?"

"You know my middle name. But I'm not sure I like the way you used it as if you're mad or something." He lifted the ring from the box and glided it on her finger. "For the record, it's an engagement ring."

"I know what it is. Where did it come from?" She held up her hand and wiggled her fingers.

"It was my Nana's."

She narrowed her eyes.

He laughed. "Not Grammy. It belonged to my mother's mom and my mom snuck it in here a little bit ago."

"Excuse me? They all knew you were okay and let me—"

"Sweetheart. Don't be mad at them. I texted my parents and asked them not to tell you right away so I could get the ring. I wanted to propose but now I realize I haven't even done that yet."

"No. You haven't." She cocked her head.

"Janelle. Will you marry me?"

"Of course I will." She leaned forward and kissed him, thankfully without crushing his chest.

Cheers erupted from the hallway.

"You've got to be kidding me." She buried her face in his neck. "Is everyone out there?"

"Yup," he said.

"And we got it on video. The whole thing," Nelson's voice echoed in the background. "Phoenix, we're going to be busting your ass for that proposal for the rest of your life."

He cupped her face. "Was it that bad?"

"Pathetic. Like I can't believe I said yes, pathetic."

"Just wait. You get to take care of me for the next month." He arched a brow.

"That's a storm I'm sure I can weather."

13

ONE YEAR LATER...

Janelle leaned against the railing, watching the sunset. It was still the most magical thing she ever saw, next to being married.

"Hey, sweetheart." Phoenix strolled across the deck carrying a bottle of wine and two glasses. "How was your day off?" He set them on the small table.

"Interesting." She turned, giving her husband of six months a big hug and kiss. "Everything good at the restaurant?"

"Easy day. No drama. No complaints. A good start to the season." He took her by the hand. "What did you do today?'

"I took Ashley to school. Spent a little time with Cole and Lilly. Had lunch with your mom and we got our nails done. And then I went to the doctor."

He jerked his head. "Is everything okay?"

"You might want a big glass of wine and be sitting down for this."

"That means I should stand." He poured a healthy glass and handed it to her.

"No. I'll pass."

"Since when have you turned down good wine?" He took a long sip.

"Well, the doctor mentioned it would be a good idea for the next seven months."

He cocked his head. "What doctor and why would they put a timeframe on..." His eyes widened. "Oh." He stumbled backward, grabbling for the chair, but missed and landed on his ass. The red wine went all over the front of his shirt.

"Are you okay?" She covered her mouth, trying to stifle her laugh, but gave up.

He stared at her. "Are you serious? I mean, we just started trying." He pushed himself to a standing position. He set the glass down and wiped his hands on his shirt.

"I'm eight weeks pregnant." She pulled out an image from her back pocket. "See that." She tapped the image.

"It looks like a blob."

"Well, that's baby number one."

He blinked. "What?"

She smiled. "This here is baby number two."

"You've got to be messing with me."

"Nope."

He grabbed the picture from her fingers. "There aren't any more little critters hiding in there, right?"

"Just the two."

"Holy shit." He raked his fingers through his hair. "Now I really need a drink."

"So do the rest of us," Maverick called as he came jogging across the sundeck with Cole on his shoulders.

Followed by Hensley and Ashley.

Then Nelson and Brandi with their little one, Lilly. Brandi was due with their second child any day now.

His parents were two steps behind them.

"Please tell me you didn't have my family record that." He leaned in and kissed her cheek.

"Payback's a bitch, honey." She smiled.

"Yeah, except I'm always the one who looks like an idiot in these videos." He glanced over his shoulder. "I guess we're having a party." He held the image up toward the sky. "Twins, huh?"

She nodded. "I'm hoping it's a boy and a girl. That way we can be done in one shot."

He batted her nose. "Nope. I'm going to want more. I can feel it in my bones."

"Figures." She laughed. "But I was thinking. If we do have one of each, do you think we could name them Jason and Anne Marie?"

Phoenix smiled. "Of course."

"Are you happy?"

"I'm thrilled and terrified all at the same time." He wrapped his arms around her. "I don't know how we're going to handle two at once."

"Same way we do everything. By driving right through the storm."

Thank you for reading *Before the Storm*. Please feel free to leave an honest review.

If you'd like to know more about our local State Trooper Stacey, her story can be found here: **Murder in Paradise Bay**

If you'd like to know more about Corbin River and the River Winery, check out: ***Corbin's Mission*** and ***Kisses Sweeter than Wine.***

Grab a glass of vino, kick back, relax, and let the romance roll in...

Sign up for my [Newsletter](https://dl.bookfunnel.com/)

82gm8b9k4y) where I often give away free books before publication.

Join my private Facebook group (https://www.facebook.com/groups/191706547909047/) where I post exclusive excerpts and discuss all things murder and love!

ABOUT THE AUTHOR

Jen Talty is the *USA Today* Bestselling Author of Contemporary Romance, Romantic Suspense, and Paranormal Romance. In the fall of 2020, her short story was selected and featured in a 1001 Dark Nights Anthology.

Regardless of the genre, her goal is to take you on a ride that will leave you floating under the sun with warmth in your heart. She writes stories about broken heroes and heroines who aren't necessarily looking for romance, but in the end, they find the kind of love books are written about :).

She first started writing while carting her kids to one hockey rink after the other, averaging 170 games per year between 3 kids in 2 countries and 5 states. Her first book, IN TWO WEEKS was originally published in 2007. In 2010 she helped form a publishing company (Cool Gus Publishing) with *NY Times* Bestselling Author Bob Mayer where she ran the technical side of the business through 2016.

Jen is currently enjoying the next phase of her life... the empty nester! She and her husband reside in Jupiter, Florida.

Grab a glass of vino, kick back, relax, and let the romance roll in...

Sign up for my [Newsletter](https://dl.bookfunnel.com/82gm8b9k4y) where I often give away free books before publication.

Join my private [Facebook group](https://www.facebook.com/groups/191706547909047/) where I post exclusive excerpts and discuss all things murder and love!

Never miss a new release. Follow me on Amazon:amazon.com/author/jentalty
And on Bookbub: bookbub.com/authors/jen-talty

ALSO BY JEN TALTY

Brand new series: SAFE HARBOR!

Mine To Keep

Mine To Save

Mine To Protect

Mine to Hold

Mine to Love

Check out LOVE IN THE ADIRONDACKS!

Shattered Dreams

An Inconvenient Flame

The Wedding Driver

Clear Blue Sky

Blue Moon

Before the Storm

NY STATE TROOPER SERIES (also set in the Adirondacks!)

In Two Weeks

Dark Water

Deadly Secrets

Murder in Paradise Bay

To Protect His own

Deadly Seduction

When A Stranger Calls

His Deadly Past

The Corkscrew Killer

First Responders: A spin-off from the NY State Troopers series

Playing With Fire

Private Conversation

The Right Groom

After The Fire

Caught In The Flames

Chasing The Fire

Legacy Series
Dark Legacy
Legacy of Lies
Secret Legacy

Emerald City

Investigate Away

Sail Away

Fly Away

Flirt Away

Colorado Brotherhood Protectors

Fighting For Esme

Defending Raven

Fay's Six

Darius' Promise

Yellowstone Brotherhood Protectors

Guarding Payton

Wyatt's Mission

Corbin's Mission

Candlewood Falls

Rivers Edge

The Buried Secret

Its In His Kiss

Lips Of An Angel

Kisses Sweeter than Wine

A Little Bit Whiskey

It's all in the Whiskey

Johnnie Walker

Georgia Moon

Jack Daniels

Jim Beam

Whiskey Sour

Whiskey Cobbler

Whiskey Smash

Irish Whiskey

The Monroes

Color Me Yours

Color Me Smart

Color Me Free

Color Me Lucky

Color Me Ice

Color Me Home

Search and Rescue

Protecting Ainsley

Protecting Clover

Protecting Olympia

Protecting Freedom

Protecting Princess

Protecting Marlowe

Fallport Rescue Operations

Searching for Madison

Searching for Haven

DELTA FORCE-NEXT GENERATION

Shielding Jolene

Shielding Aalyiah

Shielding Laine

Shielding Talullah

Shielding Maribel

Shielding Daisy

The Men of Thief Lake

Rekindled

Destiny's Dream

Federal Investigators

Jane Doe's Return

The Butterfly Murders

THE AEGIS NETWORK

The Sarich Brother

The Lighthouse

Her Last Hope

The Last Flight

The Return Home

The Matriarch

Aegis Network: Jacksonville Division

A SEAL's Honor

Aegis Network Short Stories

Max & Milian

A Christmas Miracle

Spinning Wheels

Holiday's Vacation

Special Forces Operation Alpha

Burning Desire

Burning Kiss

Burning Skies

Burning Lies

Burning Heart

Burning Bed

Remember Me Always

The Brotherhood Protectors

Out of the Wild

Rough Justice

Rough Around The Edges

Rough Ride

Rough Edge

Rough Beauty

The Brotherhood Protectors

The Saving Series

Saving Love

Saving Magnolia

Saving Leather

Hot Hunks

Cove's Blind Date Blows Up

My Everyday Hero – Ledger

Tempting Tavor

Malachi's Mystic Assignment

Needing Neor

Holiday Romances

A Christmas Getaway

Alaskan Christmas

Whispers

Christmas In The Sand

Heroes & Heroines on the Field

Taking A Risk

Tee Time

A New Dawn

The Blind Date

Spring Fling

Summers Gone

Winter Wedding

The Awakening

The Collective Order

The Lost Sister

The Lost Soldier

The Lost Soul

The Lost Connection

The New Order